Eating
Vegetarian

Eating Vegetarian

A Healthy Cookbook for Beginners

Alissa Bilden Warham
Steve Warham

ROCKRIDGE
PRESS

For general information on our other products and services or to obtain technical support, please contact our Customer Care Department within the U.S. at (866) 744-2665, or outside the U.S. at (510) 253-0500.

Rockridge Press publishes its books in a variety of electronic and print formats. Some content that appears in print may not be available in electronic books, and vice versa.

TRADEMARKS: Rockridge Press and the Rockridge Press logo are trademarks or registered trademarks of Callisto Media Inc. and/or its affiliates, in the United States and other countries, and may not be used without written permission. All other trademarks are the property of their respective owners. Rockridge Press is not associated with any product or vendor mentioned in this book.

Interior and Cover Designer: Richard Tapp
Photo Art Director/Art Manager: Megan Baggott
Editor: Lauren Ladoceour
Production Editor: Ashley Polikoff
Photography © 2020 Elysa Weitala; food styling by Victoria Woollard, except page: pp vi–vii, 14–15, 26–27, 36, 40–41, 44, 56–57, 68, 70, 74–75, 78, 82, 92, 96–97, 102, 106, 114, 122, 146, 150, 156, 160, 166
Author photo by Steve Warham

ISBN: Print 978-1-64611-646-1 | eBook 978-1-64611-647-8
R0

To the Bilden and Warham families.

You've always encouraged us to learn and grow and have never wavered in supporting us—even when we served food you weren't accustomed to.

Contents

Introduction

We're Steve and Alissa. Welcome to the wonderful world of vegetarian cooking! Like you, we were once new to vegetarianism, and we know it's not easy to make the transition—whether you're doing it for health, environmental, religious, or even political reasons. You probably have a lot of questions: How do I know what ingredients are truly vegetarian? Can I still get all my nutritional requirements without meat? Will dinner still be delicious and enjoyable? Even if you've picked up this book because you're an omnivore who lives with and cooks for someone who's a new vegetarian, the questions and pursuit are the same: making sure everyone's healthy, happy, and satisfied at the table.

The transition can be a big one, depending on how you're used to eating. Alissa grew up in eastern Montana's cattle country. Beef was a staple in her home, along with chicken and seafood. Steve is from upstate New York, where his mother lived on a dairy farm and his father worked on these same farms that were a vital part of the area's way of life.

As adults, we began to question the food choices we were raised on, especially after several family members were diagnosed with cancer, including Alissa's mom and Steve's aunt and uncle. Then, while living in New York City, Alissa received word that her dad had also been diagnosed with colorectal cancer.

It was at this moment that we both wondered if what we ate played a role in our family's history of cancer. We decided that for the two of us, it was worth experimenting with a new kind of diet—a vegetarian diet.

Regardless if you choose to follow a strict vegetarian diet or simply opt to make vegetarian meals every once in a while, consuming more plants appears to be a good decision according to almost every health study conducted. The key is to incorporate plant-based eating more often without feeling deprived. And it's completely possible—but don't just take it from us. Try it yourself!

Every recipe in this cookbook can be adapted and modified for your particular needs or for the needs of your loved ones. If a family member prefers to have a little meat, it can easily be added to many of these recipes. Every individual needs the ability to make their own choices in their own time.

We are grateful to report that both of our families are happy and healthy today. When they visit us, we serve them the food they prefer, including meat. Over the years, we have begun to see an increase in the plants that accompany their protein or even their choosing to eat completely vegetarian meals. We love it. Making any change can be difficult, but the more you're exposed to other types of food and cuisines, the more curiosity and willingness usually follows.

Wherever you or your loved ones are in your personal food journey, take it one step at a time—especially if that first step involves eating more plants. We always begin somewhere. Thanks for beginning here.

Part One

The Vegetarian Way

Chapter One

Going Vegetarian

Any significant change in one's life, and particularly one involving deep-rooted cultural traditions such as food, can feel overwhelming. When changing from a meat-based to a vegetarian diet, it might be difficult to know where to start. In this chapter, we provide helpful information and guidance on how to make this significant dietary change. It is our desire to help you in this transition because our personal journey has been such a positive experience and we wish the same for you.

Welcome to the Veg Life

You are now entering a new, creative relationship with food and cooking. This change will affect your mind, body, and, of course, what you put on your plate. It might not always be easy, but it will be worthwhile and soon feel like the new normal. Welcome to the veg life!

There have been vegetarians and vegans for centuries. Well-known historical figures—Einstein, Gandhi, Da Vinci—and many others restricted their intake of meat and believed in the power of plants. You are about to follow in their footsteps.

The word *vegetarian* was initially coined in 1842 by the founders of the British Vegetarian Society. Recently, vegetarian eating has exploded in popularity due to changing food preferences and the greater accessibility of fresh ingredients. Currently 11 percent of the world's population considers themselves vegetarian or vegan, according to a 2018 survey conducted by IPSOS Global Advisor.

There are various subcategories of vegetarianism. It's easy to find a natural fit for everyone.

FLEXITARIAN

Flexitarians consume a diet with a focus on moderation. Individuals follow a plant-based diet with the option of an occasional serving of meat. This is a great starting point for people who desire to eat healthier but would benefit from a gradual transition.

FRUITARIAN

A fruitarian diet is one in which individuals consume only fruit with occasional nuts and seeds. The belief of this approach to eating is that one should only eat food that is *produced by plants*, not the plants themselves. They believe the killing of any plant or animal is inherently wrong.

LACTO VEGETARIAN

This version of vegetarianism includes dairy, but restricts meat and eggs. This is a good option for people who love cheese. Meals can still be rich and creamy, but additional plant-based protein sources are necessary for adequate nutrition.

LACTO-OVO VEGETARIAN

By far the most common version of vegetarianism, this lifestyle choice allows one to eat mainly plants and also offers the flexibility to consume dairy and eggs.

OVO VEGETARIAN

This vegetarian diet includes eggs but no dairy is consumed. For individuals who are lactose intolerant or have an aversion to dairy, this option is a good place to start your plant-based journey.

PESCATARIAN

This diet is based on the Italian word *pesce*, which means "fish." This option enables an individual to follow a vegetarian diet with the addition of seafood. It allows one to tread the water of vegetarianism while still consuming animal protein.

RAW VEGAN

This subset of veganism promotes eating foods that are not heated above 118 degrees Fahrenheit. Like veganism (see following), it excludes all food and materials of animal origin. Followers of this sect believe consuming food that has not been cooked is higher in vitamins and nutrients.

VEGAN

A vegan diet avoids all meat, eggs, and dairy. Additionally, living a vegan lifestyle not only avoids the consumption of all animals and animal products (including honey, as it is made by bees), but is extended to exclude clothing, skincare products, and home goods made from animals or products that are tested on animals.

Please remember, it is always best to speak to a medical professional before beginning any substantial lifestyle or diet change.

IS THE VEGETARIAN DIET PRACTICAL?

IS IT EXPENSIVE?

Absolutely not. In fact, by removing meat from your grocery cart, you will save money. Fresh produce is often cheaper than processed food, and pantry staples like beans and grains can be purchased on sale or in bulk and have a longer shelf life than meats.

WILL IT TAKE MORE TIME TO COOK?

Many vegetarian meals are incredibly easy and quick to make. It is our goal to share tasty and simple recipes with you in this cookbook.

WILL I GET SICK MORE OFTEN?

No. You may actually find yourself sick less often! Most cases of food poisoning and common stomach viruses are caused by contaminated meat.

WILL I STILL BE ABLE TO DINE OUT?

Absolutely. Most restaurants today offer vegetarian and vegan options or will make one upon request.

The Health Benefits

There are numerous health benefits of a vegetarian diet when compared to a traditional meat-based diet. A great amount of research has been done regarding the benefits of eating more fruits, vegetables, and grains compared to animal protein. Here is a snapshot of some of the health benefits you can expect while limiting your consumption of meat. Feel free to search for further information about benefits you are bound to experience. See the References section (page 187) for further information.

NUTRITIONAL BOOST

Our bodies were made to consume whole foods that grow in the ground, on trees, and all other ways that natural food is grown. Therefore, when we eat food grown by Mother Earth, our bodies respond positively with a burst of energy and vitality we never feel when consuming processed manmade food. Trust how your body feels!

DIGESTIVE HEALTH

According to Johns Hopkins School of Medicine, most doctors agree that a large percentage of people are not consuming adequate fiber and this adversely affects our digestive health. Foods that are naturally more prevalent while following a vegetarian diet, like leafy greens, whole grains, and some fruits including avocados, are all beneficial to one's digestive health due to their high fiber content.

Reasons People Go Vegetarian

There are many reasons people choose a vegetarian diet. Many decide to do so for *health* reasons or after a recommendation from a physician to lower cholesterol. Others choose a similar path because they love animals, advocating for *animal rights*, or a desire to decrease their impact on *environmental concerns* including global warming. Vegetarianism is not a new concept. Cultures all over the world have been eating a vegetarian diet based on their *religious beliefs* for centuries.

HEART DISEASE PROTECTION

Excess fat and cholesterol consumption has been found to lead to the hardening of arteries and a rise in cholesterol within the blood, according to *The China Study*. Both of these health concerns often lead to heart disease and, possibly, heart attacks. Only animal protein contains cholesterol as well as high levels of saturated fat. By consuming a vegetarian diet without these contributors, heart disease can even be reversed.

LOWERED CANCER RISK

According to the World Cancer Research Fund/American Institute for Cancer Research, there is evidence that a vegetarian diet with an increased level of fiber consumption, antioxidants, and other phytochemicals that are prevalent in fruits and vegetables, helps maintain a healthy weight and reduce the risk of cancer in individuals.

BLOOD GLUCOSE

Processed foods and carbohydrates are found to have an elevated level of added sugar. When consuming these foods in abundance over a long period, they can affect how the body regulates blood sugar levels and possibly lead to type 2 diabetes, according to the

WHAT ABOUT KIDS?

WILL MY CHILD BE HEALTHY ON A VEGETARIAN DIET?

Children all over the world have been following vegetarian diets throughout human history. People who follow a vegetarian diet often are healthier, according to *The China Study* by Colin T. Campbell. The key is consuming a well-balanced diet of ALL types of plants, nuts, seeds, and grains.

WILL MY CHILD GET ENOUGH PROTEIN?

Absolutely. If a child has a well-rounded vegetarian diet, they will consume a similar protein intake as their meat-eating peers.

WILL MY CHILD LIKE THE FOOD?

Yes. Most children love fruits and vegetables. For pickier eaters, a slow transition incorporating more vegetables into their already favorite meals can be helpful. For example, adding veggies to homemade macaroni and cheese.

American Diabetes Association. By eating a whole foods vegetarian diet, these risks are lowered.

COGNITIVE HEALTH

Many foods consumed on a vegetarian diet promote cognitive health and functioning. Some of these foods include green leafy vegetables, berries, tea or coffee, and walnuts. By eating these foods regularly, you can help maintain or improve brain health and cognitive functioning, according to Harvard Medical School.

BONE DENSITY

Our bones naturally lose density as we age, which can lead to osteoporosis. A lack of calcium, especially for an extended period of time, can play a role in the development of osteoporosis, according to the Mayo Clinic. Consuming calcium and adequate plant-based protein, helps promote an increase in bone density and healthier bones.

WEIGHT MANAGEMENT

Adhering to a vegetarian diet can help you maintain a healthy weight. Eating an abundance of whole grains, lean protein sources, and vegetables helps us maintain or even lose weight. It is possible, however, to see a weight gain initially during the transition to a vegetarian diet if you merely replace animal protein with carbs and cheese.

Nutritional Considerations

There are some nutrients that can be more difficult to get while following a vegetarian diet. To avoid any deficiencies, eat well-balanced meals that consist of a variety of foods. Here are some deficiencies to be aware of while eating a plant-based diet.

CALORIES

Food is life. It is important to consume the recommended number of calories based on your gender, age, and body type, keeping in mind that adjustments may be needed based on your activity level.

PROTEIN

Vital protein intake can be sustained through a vegetarian diet, despite the belief by many that protein is only found in meat sources. Adequate protein can be consumed through plants, but it is important to include a range of protein sources to meet your body's needs. Vegetarians need to eat a diet with nuts, seeds, grains, and eggs. Additionally, plant-based proteins such as tofu and tempeh can be consumed to meet one's recommended daily protein levels.

WHAT ARE MY DAILY NUTRITIONAL REQUIREMENTS?

The following are daily nutritional requirements according to the U.S. Department of Health and Human Services. Please remember that these are guidelines, and that it is always best to consult your personal physician if you are concerned or have additional questions.

	Men	Women	Adolescents	Young Children
Calories	2,000 to 3,000	1,600 to 2,400	1,800 to 3,200	1,000 to 1,600
Protein	56g	46g	34 to 52g	13 to 19g
Fat (% of Total Cals)	20 to 35	20 to 35	25 to 35	30 to 35
Calcium	1,000mg	1,000mg	1,300mg	700 to 1,300mg
Vitamin D	600 IU	600 IU	600 IU	600 IU
Vitamin B$_{12}$	2.4 mcg	2.4 mcg	2.4 mcg	0.9 to 1.8 mcg
Zinc	11 mg	8 mg	9 to 11mg	3 to 8mg

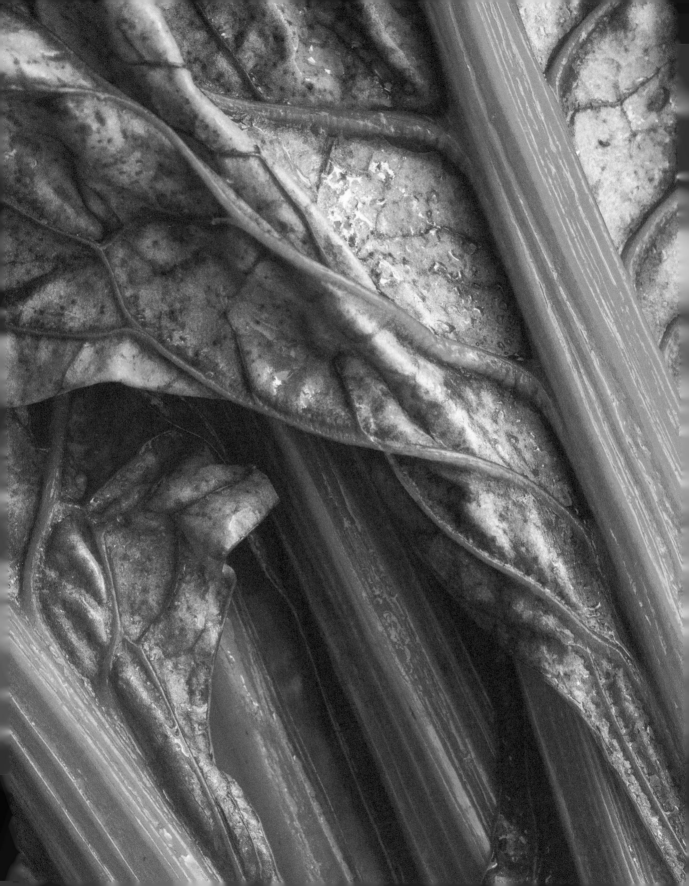

Chapter Two

The Vegetarian Kitchen

Now that you have a clearer understanding of the health benefits from adopting a vegetarian diet, it's time to learn some of the basics to set yourself up for a successful transition to vegetarian cooking at home.

There are a few essential kitchen tools, ingredients, and cooking tips that can help make your initial adjustment smoother. Learning the basics of prepping food can be a game changer when you are making meals from scratch and want to save time and avoid stress.

In this chapter, we guide you through the essentials of a well-equipped vegetarian home kitchen. This will allow you to focus on the FOOD and help you prepare delicious and satisfying recipes everyone in your household will love and request time and again.

Kitchen Tools

If you regularly prepare meals in your kitchen, we have terrific news! You most likely already own all you need to prepare tasty vegetarian meals. However, there are some useful tools and appliances that can be helpful in a vegetarian kitchen. Here are a few recommendations.

PRESSURE COOKER

One way to shave time off meal preparation is with an electric or stovetop pressure cooker. This device is able to cook vegetables and grains quickly. Electric pressure cookers have recently become popular and can often be found reasonably priced or on sale.

SPIRALIZER

This simple tool can produce creative alternatives to ordinary recipes. Almost any root vegetable, as well as squash, can be spiralized quickly to provide a low-carb alternative to pasta or a fresh idea for a salad. Yet spiralizers are compact so they use very little space in your kitchen.

BLENDER

Sometimes you just have to blend! Either a countertop blender or immersion blender can be useful when cooking vegetarian meals. Puréed soups, sauces, and condiments can be turned quickly into creamy smooth goodness. Immersion blenders are a more economical route for a beginner, but high-quality refurbished blenders may also be an option.

FOOD PROCESSOR

This useful appliance can chop, purée, grate, or blend. If you like hummus, this workhorse will be your new best friend. The larger the processor, the more useful it will be. Therefore, if you are considering purchasing this appliance, it's better to get a larger model.

Y-PEELER

This simple gadget gets the job done. Unlike a typical vegetable peeler, a Y-peeler has a larger blade that allows you to peel everything from a potato to a winter squash quickly. It is also more comfortable to hold in your hand than a traditional peeler.

CHEF'S KNIFE

When you have lots of vegetables to chop, a quality knife is a necessity. A chef's knife is the ideal size for chopping anything from fresh herbs to large squash. As an additional tip, remember to sharpen knives often. It will make all the difference when chopping.

WOK

A large wok is perfect for a quick weeknight stir-fry or sautéing large amounts of vegetables. The taller sides of the pan help prevent food from falling out when stirring and the surface is ideal for cooking at high temperatures without the worry of burning food.

ENAMELED CAST-IRON COOKWARE

This cookware might be a splurge but it is worth the investment for its versatility. Not only can you make casseroles, soups, and frittatas in it, but also homemade bread. Enameled cast-iron cookware is also incredibly easy to clean and goes from stovetop to oven to table.

RICE COOKER

This appliance may seem frivolous if you have limited storage space. We felt the same, until we purchased one. We use it all the time and never worry about overcooking the rice while we are busy preparing an entrée. Most rice cookers double as steaming baskets as well.

STEAMING BASKET

Steaming vegetables is a great method for encouraging finicky children or adults to eat more veggies if they haven't yet developed a taste for them raw. Steaming baskets are also great for steaming premade dumplings or buns.

Your New Favorite Ingredients

When beginning anything new, especially a diet, there are bound to be challenges. A new diet often involves restricting or removing a particular food or type of food. On the Atkins diet, you restrict carbs. On Paleo, you restrict grains, legumes, and dairy. With a vegetarian diet, you restrict meat. Although it might be challenging at first, as you become familiar with vegetarian guidelines, it will become significantly easier.

The most difficult part of anything new is making it a part of your regular routine. This means deciding which ingredients are best so you are able to shop smartly and affordably. We have created an ingredient checklist to help you get started with your new vegetarian diet.

POWERFUL PROTEINS

Tofu is usually one plant-based protein people initially dislike. The first time we had tofu in miso soup, it seemed tasteless. We quickly learned that by using seasonings, any plant-based protein can taste even better than meat. In fact, now we LOVE tofu. Here are some protein sources to try while following a vegetarian diet.

BEANS: This quick and easy protein source can be added to salads, soups, puréed into dips like hummus, or added to macaroni and cheese.

EXTRA-FIRM TOFU: Dice it up fine or crumble it into your skillet for vegan scrambled eggs, or chop and add it to anything that calls for chopped chicken.

HEMP OR CHIA SEEDS: These tiny seeds can be sprinkled on salads or added to smoothies. Chia seeds can also be used to make a healthy pudding by soaking the seeds overnight with any milk, or used as the binding agent for homemade seed crackers.

LENTILS: This is a great protein to add to soups and stews, or simply season cooked lentils and serve them over rice for a quick, protein-rich meal. Lentils can also mimic ground beef for sloppy joes or veggie burgers.

NUTS: Cashews or any nut may be added to salads, pastas, roasted squash, or blended into a creamy cheese-like purée. Nuts are a simple, healthy fat and protein at its best.

QUINOA: This Mayan staple is great for replacing rice as a stir-fry or curry base. It may be added to salads, Buddha bowls, casseroles, or used as a filling for stuffed peppers or zucchini boats.

SEITAN: This plant-based meat replacement is made from vital wheat

Dinner Guest Etiquette

It can feel overwhelming when initially beginning a dietary change with restrictions, especially when you're a dinner guest at someone else's house. When in doubt, ask what ingredients were used and if animal products were used, and politely apologize but state that due to your new diet, you unfortunately won't be able to eat a particular item. However, if there's food you can eat, be extra-complimentary and appreciative. We have found people to be incredibly supportive of our choices. Additionally, if it is a dinner party, offer to bring a shareable dish you can enjoy with everyone.

gluten and mimics meat in texture and look. It can be cut into small pieces for a meat-free Mongolian "beef," thinly sliced for sandwiches, or seasoned and baked into a meatless jerky.

TEMPEH: This fermented plant-based protein is great for the gut and is incredibly versatile. Crumble it for a ground meat alternative in pasta sauces and nachos, or slice and sauté it for stir-fries, wraps, or tacos.

EVERYDAY VEGETABLES

There are many vegetables you can indulge in as a vegetarian but here are a few of the most versatile veggies.

BEETS: These flavorful root veggies are naturally sweet and a great addition to salads, especially when goat cheese or other tart cheeses are used.

CARROTS: Naturally sweet and full of beta-carotene, enjoy carrots raw, roasted, or juiced for a delicious and healthy treat.

CAULIFLOWER AND BROCCOLI: Great as a raw snack with dip, or sautéed or roasted to incorporate in any entrée. These vegetables may also be riced or mashed for a lower-carb option to replace rice or mashed potatoes.

CORN: Not only is this vegetable delicious when eaten from the cob, but it's also a great frozen veggie to have on

WHAT'S THE DEAL WITH ORGANIC?

Awareness of how food affects the environment and our health has brought the popularity of organic food to the forefront. A French study was conducted in 2018 by Julia Baudry, author and a researcher with the Center of Research in Epidemiology and Statistics, Université Sorbonne Paris Cité of the French National Institute of Health and Medical Research. It found that people who consumed organic food had 25 percent fewer cancers than those who did not consume organic fruit, vegetables, dairy, and other foods. The study included and followed 70,000 adults for five years and was paid for by public and government funds.

There are several reasons for choosing organic foods. These include the option to reduce your exposure to the heavy use of pesticides in traditional farming practices, eco-consciousness, and research that shows one's health may be improved.

hand for stir-fries, Mexican meals, casseroles, or to add to pasta or a salad.

EGGPLANT: This Mediterranean ingredient may be roasted, fried, or stewed to give a plant-based meaty texture to countless entrées.

HEARTY GREENS: Great raw in a healthy chopped salad, wilted as a nutritious addition to pasta or egg bakes, or steamed for a low-carb sandwich wrap, versatility is the name of the game here.

PEPPERS: Sweet or spicy, small or large—all types of peppers are a great vegetable option to keep handy for snacking or to use as a main ingredient in many cuisines.

POTATOES: A budget-friendly ingredient that's both filling and versatile. Simply bake and top for a weeknight meal, chop and add to soups and curries, or mash or fry for comforting homemade nourishment.

SQUASH: Readily available in every season, this veggie can be roasted, puréed, or stuffed for an elegant main course. Additionally, it can be chopped and frozen for easy weeknight meal prep.

HEALTHY FATS

Our bodies, especially our brains, require healthy fats, including omega-3s, to live and thrive. A typical dietary source of these fats is salmon, but for vegetarians, these can be found in plant-based options like avocados, nuts and seeds, or oils such as coconut, olive, or sunflower. Eggs are also a great option for providing healthy omega-3s.

In this cookbook, you will find recipes that provide these healthy fats. It is important to note that many of these healthy foods also tend to be high in calories, so portion moderation is key.

HEARTY CARBS

Carbohydrates are the energy source for our bodies. However, not all carbs are created equal. It is vital to eat a majority of carbs that are whole grain and protein rich. The following are some carbs worth exploring.

BEANS OR LEGUMES: Black beans, chickpeas, lentils, mung beans, peanuts, peas, and others are healthy carbs that are also protein heavy. These pantry staples are economical and a great addition to almost every meatless meal.

HIGH-FIBER PASTA: A quick and filling carb for easy weeknight pasta, salads, or air-fried crackers. Be sure to check out protein-rich lentil, chickpea, or mung bean pasta now available in most grocery stores.

OATS: Think beyond your morning oatmeal. Oats can be soaked overnight for a fuss-free breakfast on the go, or combined with savory ingredients for a filling lunch or dinner.

QUINOA: This high-fiber and protein-rich carb is easy to prepare and has a nutty flavor that pairs well with everything from greens to spicy stir-fries.

RICE: Opt for brown rice over white rice for a healthier kitchen staple that can be used for stuffing and frying, or as a base for vegetable-rich curries.

SWEET POTATO: This tasty spud is great baked or it can be used for a sweet pie filling or to make a healthy pudding. It can also be shredded and mixed with a favorite sauce for a zesty meat-free sandwich.

Produce Prep 101

One often discovers new ways to use a variety of vegetables when cooking vegetarian. However, one also may discover that vegetables can take a significant amount of time to prepare. Here are a few tricks to save time when prepping some common vegetables. Find more on page 174.

WASHING LEAFY GREENS

Dirt and impurities can be caught between the leaves in most greens. Pull the leaves off the core and wash them thoroughly with cold water. Chop the greens and use a salad spinner to

ARE FROZEN FRUITS AND VEGETABLES HEALTHY?

Fresh is always best, but one of the easiest and most cost-effective ways to purchase fruits and vegetables is frozen. The fruits and vegetables can be picked and frozen until ready for use, requiring no extra sugar or other added ingredients.

Canned vegetables have fewer nutrients than frozen, because canning involves cooking. Removing the skin of fruits and vegetables and the water used during processing can remove additional mineral content as well.

According to Harvard Health, fiber, protein, carbohydrate, and mineral content do not differ significantly between frozen and fresh produce. However, the longer fresh sits, whether in transit or on the shelf, nutrients are lost. So if you can't buy fresh-picked local, frozen fruits and veggies are the next best thing.

remove excess water or let dry before adding any dressings or sauces.

HALVING BUTTERNUT SQUASH

Wash the squash. Using a chef's knife, lightly pierce the skin of the butternut to create a fine line where you plan to cut. With a firm motion, begin to cut the butternut, leaving the stem end for last. Use a towel for grip, if necessary.

PITTING AVOCADOS

Wash the exterior of the avocado. Use a knife to cut the avocado from top to bottom and back up the other side to the top again, letting the knife's edge meet the pit without cutting into it. Twist the two halves of the avocado to separate them. Using a sharp knife, strike the pit and lift it from the flesh. Slice the avocado into thin slices or chunks. Then, use a large spoon to scoop the flesh out of the skin.

SEEDING BELL PEPPERS

Wash the exterior of the pepper thoroughly. Using a cutting board and a sharp knife, cut off the top ½ inch of the pepper. This removes the stem and exposes the core and seeds. Next, cut the bottom ¼ inch off the pepper. This section is sometimes bitter. Slice down one side of the pepper, exposing the core. Remove the core, seeds, and white veins with your knife, rolling the pepper as you go. Continue cutting the pepper as directed in the recipe.

ROASTING BEETS

Preheat the oven to 400° F. Cut the stems off the beets if they still have them. Scrub the outside of each beet under running water using a vegetable brush. Once clean, place the beets into a pie dish and fill it with 1 inch of water. Tightly cover the pie dish with aluminum foil. Roast for 40 to 45 minutes. Remove from the oven and let cool. Rub the beets with clean hands under warm running water to remove the skin. Use immediately or refrigerate in a sealed container for up to 2 weeks.

CORING CAULIFLOWER

Remove any green leaves from the bottom of the cauliflower. Flip the cauliflower upside down on a cutting board. Using a very sharp knife, cut into the cauliflower at an inward angle around the stem. Once you have cut around the stem, the core should be loose enough to remove by hand. After the cauliflower is cored, rinse it well under cool water and separate the florets.

Delicious Flavors

There's a misconception that food without meat lacks flavor. This could not be further from the truth. Many

WHAT ARE SOME LOW-CARB SWAPS?

CAULIFLOWER RICE: One of the most versatile veggies, it can be riced, whipped, cut into steaks, or roasted whole. Rice and top with easy stir-fries or create homemade low-carb vegetable sushi.

CABBAGE NOODLES: Chop any cabbage finely for a rice or noodle replacement or mix it with a peanut sauce for a new version of pad thai.

LETTUCE WRAPS: Steamed collard greens can be used to replace tortillas for a low-carb sandwich wrap; use endive or another small green leaf and fill with chopped vegetables and quinoa for an appetizer or side.

SHIRATAKI NOODLES: These thin transparent noodles are from Japan. They are a low-carb option for ramen, Thai noodle dishes, and pasta.

SPAGHETTI SQUASH: This unique winter squash naturally shreds into fine noodle-like strands with just the scrape of a fork. Use in place of any pasta dish that traditionally calls for thin noodles.

SPIRALIZED NOODLES: Think beyond zucchini noodles, or zoodles. Spiralize any root vegetable (beet, carrot, daikon, rutabaga, and turnip) for a new take on low-carb noodles.

vegetarian meals explode with vibrant flavors from the variety of vegetables and seasonings used.

There are some key pantry items used often in meat-free recipes, including in the recipes in this cookbook. You may need to purchase some of them before starting to cook, but you will use them again and again. Here are some vegetarian essentials we suggest you keep stocked in your kitchen:

COCONUT MILK: This creamy milk will be used in more than Thai recipes. Coconut rice, chia pudding, curries, soups, and ice creams are just a few ways to use this versatile milk.

LIQUID AMINOS OR SOY SAUCE: These zesty and savory liquids will be used for far more than dipping sushi—think stir-fries, sauces, and marinating tofu.

SPICES AND DRIED HERBS: Spices you may want to keep on hand include ground cumin, ground coriander, smoked paprika, and ground ginger. As for dried herbs, basil, dill, oregano, rosemary, and thyme are the basics. However, experiment with others you might like, such as lavender, marjoram, mint, and tarragon.

TAHINI: This sauce is made from toasted ground hulled sesame seeds. It's a key ingredient in hummus and baba ghanoush, but it may be used as a flavorful drizzle on sandwiches and wraps, or even added to cookie dough for an extra-rich nutty flavor.

VEGETABLE BROTH: This flavorful broth is used in soups, dips, stir-fries, and more. It can also be made at home with leftover produce. You will want to keep this essential on hand.

10 Tips for Picky Eaters

Starting anything new can result in anxiety. When you initially prepare vegetarian meals, there will be new ingredients to explore along with many classics. It's understandable to be wary of new foods and ingredients. To help ease the transition for everyone, here are some tips that can benefit even the pickiest of eaters.

1. **START SLOW.** It sometime helps to ease into a new diet gradually. Begin by cooking meatless meals on Monday. Then try to add three or four vegetarian meals a week.

2. **BE CREATIVE WITH PRESENTATION.** Make your meals appetizing and fun, especially for young children. Try adding a face to a veggie pizza or calling stuffed zucchini, zucchini "boats."

3. **BEGIN WITH SMALL AMOUNTS.** Try a single bite or two and then slowly transition into eating a full serving.

4. **DISGUISE OR HIDE.** Particularly with vegetables and greens within an easier-to-eat entrée like pasta.

5. **INVOLVE PICKY EATERS IN MEAL PLANNING AND COOKING.** By involving others, you increase the odds they will eat and enjoy meatless meals.

6. **GET OUT OF THE KITCHEN.** It might be helpful to go to a new restaurant to further encourage yourself and others to branch out.

7. **PAY ATTENTION TO TEXTURE.** For example, rather than serving whole tomatoes right away, try them in a puréed sauce first, then a chunky sauce, and finally serve whole tomatoes within a main course.

8. **BE PATIENT WITH NEW FOODS.** Experts say it often takes 11 tries to accept something new. Even if it's not an immediate love, it doesn't mean that

OVERFLOWING SPRING ROLLS
WITH **PEANUT SATAY SAUCE**

SERVES 4 to 6
PREP TIME: 15 minutes
COOK TIME: 10 minutes

FOR THE SPRING ROLLS

8 spring roll rice paper wrappers

2 carrots, cut into small slivers

2 scallions, thinly sliced

1 avocado, peeled, pitted, and
thinly sliced

1 cucumber, peeled and cut into
small slivers

1 cup microgreens, sprouts, or
chopped lettuce

1 bunch fresh mint, stemmed

FOR THE PEANUT SATAY SAUCE

½ cup creamy peanut butter

¼ cup water

3 tablespoons soy sauce, or
liquid aminos

2 teaspoons sriracha, or chili sauce

2 teaspoons freshly squeezed
lime juice

1 teaspoon maple syrup

Spring rolls are a quick and easy appetizer or snack packed or overflowing in this case, with fresh raw vegetables. The combination of veggies can also be adjusted according to your preference or what you have on hand. The element that takes these simple rolls to the next level is the peanut satay sauce. It's creamy, rich, and perfect for dipping.

TO MAKE THE SPRING ROLLS

1. Fill a shallow dish with hot water. If the water cools, replace it with warm water, which works best.

2. Submerge a dry spring roll wrapper in the water, moving it around gently with your fingertips. The wrapper will begin to soften. When it is completely soft, remove it from the water carefully with both hands. Try not to tear it; it will be delicate. Place it on a clean plate.

3. In the center of the soft wrapper, place some of the carrot, scallions, avocado, cucumber, microgreens, and mint. About ½ cup of ingredients will fit in each wrapper.

4. Wrap up the spring roll like a cone or fold it like a burrito, wrapping both ends to form a completely enclosed package. Repeat with the remaining wrappers and filling ingredients.

CONTINUED

TO MAKE THE PEANUT SATAY SAUCE

5. In a saucepan over medium-low heat, combine the peanut butter, water, soy sauce, sriracha, lime juice, and maple syrup.

6. Cook, stirring frequently, for 1 to 2 minutes until the mixture thickens slightly into a sauce. Serve alongside the spring rolls for dipping.

MAKE IT EASIER To save time, hoisin sauce can also be used for dipping. It is a Chinese sauce made from soybeans with a sweet and salty taste that goes great with the raw vegetable filling.

PER SERVING Calories: 327; Total fat: 23g; Carbohydrates: 20g; Fiber: 6g; Protein: 12g; Calcium: 65mg; Vitamin D: 0mcg; Vitamin B12: 0mcg; Iron: 2mg; Zinc: 1.5mg

CHILI GARLIC TOFU JERKY

SERVES 8 to 10
PREP TIME: 15 minutes
COOK TIME: 4 hours

1 (14-ounce) package extra-firm
   tofu, drained
3 tablespoons liquid aminos, or
   soy sauce
4 dashes liquid smoke
1 tablespoon garlic powder
2 teaspoons chili powder
2 teaspoons smoked paprika
¼ teaspoon salt
¼ teaspoon freshly ground
   black pepper

MIX IT UP Vegetarian jerky can be made with other ingredients as well. Mushrooms provide a nice texture that replicates meat, or seitan. Dehydrating the jerky is another option. If you have a dehydrator, simply set it to 175° F and let the tofu dry for 4 to 6 hours, flipping halfway through the dehydrating time.

This meatless jerky tastes surprisingly like the real thing. The baked tofu is covered with a mixture of chili powder and garlic, along with liquid smoke (available in the spice aisle). Two teaspoons ground chipotle or two extra teaspoons smoked paprika are good substitutes if liquid smoke isn't available. Either way, you'll have a healthy and protein-packed snack that satisfies.

1. Preheat the oven to 250° F. Line a baking sheet with parchment paper. Set aside.
2. Wrap the tofu in a few paper towels and place it between two heavy cutting boards for 10 minutes to drain. This will help the tofu absorb the spices.
3. While the tofu drains, in a small bowl, whisk the liquid aminos and liquid smoke. Set aside.
4. In another small bowl, stir together the garlic powder, chili powder, paprika, salt, and pepper. Set aside.
5. Unwrap the tofu and cut it into very thin, long rectangles. Place them in a single layer on a clean, flat surface. Using a pastry brush or spoon, apply the liquid mixture to both sides of the tofu.
6. One at a time, dip each piece of tofu into the spice mix, making sure they are completely coated. Place the coated tofu in a single layer on the prepared baking sheet.
7. Bake for 3 to 4 hours, checking periodically and flipping 2 or 3 times for even baking. Remove when the jerky is firm and dry. Store in an airtight container for up to 2 weeks.

PER SERVING Calories: 55; Total fat: 3g; Carbohydrates: 3g; Fiber: 1g; Protein: 6g; Calcium: 91mg; Vitamin D: 0mcg; Vitamin B12: 0mcg; Iron: 1mg; Zinc: 1mg

Once sliced and plated,
these beautiful vegetables
are ready to be dressed
and garnished
with toppings.

ROOT VEGETABLE CARPACCIO WITH FETA

SERVES 4
PREP TIME: 15 minutes

3 radishes, washed and stem
ends trimmed

2 carrots, washed and stem
ends trimmed

1 red beet, washed and stem
end trimmed

1 golden beet, washed and stem
end trimmed

½ cup fresh parsley leaves,
roughly chopped

1 tablespoon pepitas

¼ cup crumbled feta

Sea salt

1 teaspoon balsamic vinegar

Carpaccio is traditionally made with beef, but this root vegetable carpaccio is a light appetizer, side, or snack that's beautiful and also nutritious. Root vegetables are often roasted, but they can also be enjoyed raw, as in this recipe. The key is to slice them extra-thin, almost as thin as paper. A mandoline is highly recommended, but a sharp chef's knife will also work. Topped with feta, pepitas, coarse salt, and balsamic vinegar, this dish is colorful and absolutely mouthwatering.

1. Using a mandoline or a very sharp knife, cut the radishes, carrots, and beets into paper-thin slices. Transfer to a large bowl and toss with the parsley. Arrange the sliced vegetables on a serving plate.
2. Top with the pepitas, feta, and salt.
3. Lightly drizzle with balsamic vinegar.
4. Refrigerate leftovers in an airtight container for 2 to 3 days.

MIX IT UP The beets can also be roasted for a sweeter variation. Wash and clean the beets and roast them in a 400° F oven for 35 to 40 minutes until tender. Cool, slice, and prepare the carpaccio as instructed.

PER SERVING Calories: 63; Total fat: 3g; Carbohydrates: 8g; Fiber: 2g; Protein: 3g; Calcium: 64mg; Vitamin D: 0mcg; Vitamin B12: 0mcg; Iron: 1mg; Zinc: 1mg

LOADED MEDITERRANEAN EGGPLANT FRIES

SERVES 3 or 4
PREP TIME: 20 minutes
COOK TIME: 30 minutes

1 large or 2 medium eggplants, peeled
   and cut into French fry–like sticks
¼ teaspoon salt
¼ teaspoon freshly ground
   black pepper
1 large tomato, diced small
1 red onion, diced small
1 Persian cucumber, diced small
¼ cup Kalamata olives, chopped
½ teaspoon ground cumin
½ teaspoon dried thyme
1 cup oat flour, plus more as needed
1 cup almond milk, plus more
   as needed
1 cup cornmeal, plus more as needed
⅓ cup hummus
1 bunch fresh parsley, stemmed and
   roughly chopped

Eggplant retains a lot of water, so don't skip the salting process, which draws out the moisture and helps the flour and cornmeal mixture to adhere better to the fries. This also makes the fries extra-crispy when baked, which is closer to traditional potato fries. Whatever you do, don't skimp on the hummus and toppings. They bring this light snack to a satisfying dish.

1. Place the eggplant sticks into a large bowl and season with salt and pepper. Set aside.
2. In another bowl, stir together the tomato, onion, cucumber, olives, cumin, and thyme. Set aside to let the flavors blend.
3. Preheat the oven to 400° F. Line a baking sheet with parchment paper.
4. Place the oat flour, almond milk, and cornmeal each in a separate medium bowl for dredging the eggplant pieces.
5. One at a time, coat each eggplant stick first in oat flour, second in the almond milk, and third in the cornmeal to coat. Place the coated fries on the prepared baking sheet well spaced out so they do not stick together. You may need to use more flour and milk to cover all the fries.
6. Bake for 20 to 30 minutes, flipping the fries halfway through the baking time, until they are golden brown.

7. Plate the cooked fries and immediately top with the vegetable mixture, along with dollops of hummus and chopped parsley. Serve warm immediately.

MIX IT UP These eggplant fries can easily be adapted for other cuisines and flavors. Change out the vegetable-and-olive mixture for a fresh basil and tomato combo for an Italian flair, or use corn, beans, and cilantro for a Tex-Mex variation.

PER SERVING Calories: 423; Total fat: 10g; Carbohydrates: 74g; Fiber: 16g; Protein: 14g; Calcium: 234mg; Vitamin D: 31mcg; Vitamin B12: 1mcg; Iron: 5mg; Zinc: 4mg

The Deal with Cholesterol

Cholesterol is a substance made in the liver that is essential to human life. However, dietary choices can cause the body to produce "bad" cholesterol that can cause excess plaque to form in the arteries, which may cause coronary heart disease, heart attacks, or strokes. Only animal-based foods contain cholesterol, so plants are naturally cholesterol-free. Therefore, vegetarians and vegans often have much lower cholesterol levels than those who eat a typical meat-based diet.

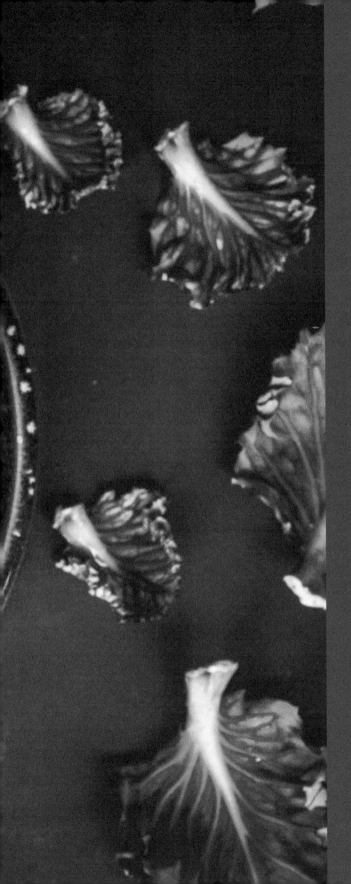

Chapter Four

Salads

HEARTS OF PALM POMEGRANATE SALAD

SERVES 4 to 6
PREP TIME: 20 minutes

1 bunch fresh cilantro, stemmed
2 tablespoons apple cider vinegar
1 tablespoon spicy mustard
1 tablespoon sugar or coconut sugar
¼ cup olive oil, plus more as needed
1 pound Brussels sprouts, shredded
   (using a mandoline or knife)
1 bunch arugula
1 mango, julienned
1 avocado, peeled, pitted, and cut
   into slices
1 pomegranate, seeded
1 (14-ounce) can hearts of
   palm, chopped

Brussels sprouts are highly nutritious, especially when eaten raw, providing lots of fiber as well as vitamins C and K. But the nutrition doesn't stop there. This salad also has heart-healthy avocado and arugula as well as mango, hearts of palm, and pomegranate arils. The sprouts are shaved or chopped into small pieces to offer a satisfying crunch.

1. In a food processor or blender, combine the cilantro, vinegar, mustard, and sugar. With the motor running, slowly drizzle in the olive oil until it is the desired consistency. Set aside.
2. In a large bowl, combine the Brussels sprouts and arugula. Give this a quick mix to blend.
3. Add the mango, avocado, pomegranate seeds, and hearts of palm to the Brussels sprouts.
4. Drizzle the dressing over the salad and serve.
5. Refrigerate leftovers in an airtight container for 3 to 4 days.

SUBSTITUTION Instead of pomegranate seeds, dried cranberries or raisins are also delicious. The mango can also be replaced by oranges or another fruit of your choice.

PER SERVING Calories: 344; Total fat: 21g; Carbohydrates: 39g; Fiber: 12g; Protein: 8g; Calcium: 128mg; Vitamin D: 0mcg; Vitamin B12: 0mcg; Iron: 5mg; Zinc: 2mg

PEAR AND FENNEL PASTA SALAD

SERVES 4 to 6
PREP TIME: 20 minutes
COOK TIME: 5 minutes

1 cup hazelnuts
1 pound gluten-free elbow macaroni, or similar pasta, cooked according to the package directions and drained
1 bunch arugula
1 fennel bulb, chopped
2 pears, cut into slices
½ head radicchio, sliced
⅓ cup crumbled goat cheese
1 bunch fresh dill
Juice of 1 lemon
Olive oil, for dressing (optional)

This is not your typical pasta salad. Instead of the traditional high-calorie, high-fat, low-nutrition version, this one combines pasta and goat cheese with fresh arugula, fennel, and radicchio for added flavor and crunch along with fiber and vitamins A, C, and K. The hazelnuts provide a nutty flavor and protein. Finally, the fresh pear and dill add a touch of elegance.

1. In a dry skillet over medium heat, toast the hazelnuts for 4 to 5 minutes, stirring occasionally until the skins start to turn dark brown and the nuts become fragrant.
2. In a large bowl, combine the cooked pasta, arugula, fennel, pears, radicchio, goat cheese, dill, and hazelnuts. Toss to combine.
3. Serve with a splash of lemon juice and a little olive oil, if desired.
4. Refrigerate leftovers in an airtight container for 2 to 3 days.

ANIMAL STYLE Thinly sliced prosciutto can be added to this salad to meet the needs of all members of your family. Simply make the pasta salad and divide into serving portions before incorporating the ham.

PER SERVING Calories: 738; Total fat: 25g; Carbohydrates: 110g; Fiber: 12g; Protein: 23g; Calcium: 136mg; Vitamin D: 0mcg; Vitamin B12: 0mcg; Iron: 6mg; Zinc: 3mg

Load up this completely customizable panzanella with your favorite mix-and-match ingredients.

FRESH SUMMER PANZANELLA

SERVES 4 to 6
PREP TIME: 20 minutes
COOK TIME: 15 minutes

¼ cup olive oil

2 tablespoons red wine vinegar

½ teaspoon garlic powder

½ teaspoon dried basil

½ teaspoon salt

¼ teaspoon freshly ground
    black pepper

2 slices crusty bread, cut into
    1-inch cubes

Olive oil, for drizzling

6 asparagus stalks, woody ends
    trimmed, cut into bite-size
    pieces (optional)

1 cup trimmed, chopped sugar
    snap peas (optional)

5 to 6 cups arugula, or lettuce of choice

1 zucchini, cut into ribbons (optional)

1 cup cherry tomatoes or 2 medium
    tomatoes, sliced

1 red onion, sliced

½ cup olives

6 ounces fresh mozzarella cheese, cut
    into bite-size pieces (optional)

¼ cup fresh basil, torn or chopped

This panzanella allows summer's bounty to shine. Panzanella is a Tuscan salad that includes crusty, stale bread, which is chopped, baked, and then rehydrated with the dressing. Although the vegetable list is long, it can be reduced to fit your family's tastes and preferences. This easily becomes a full meal by adding a protein such as chickpeas, chopped tofu, or even grilled chicken for the carnivores in your family.

1. In a small bowl, whisk the olive oil, vinegar, garlic powder, basil, salt, and pepper until combined. Set aside.

2. Preheat the oven to 350° F. Meanwhile, bring a large pot of slightly salted water to a boil over high heat.

3. Spread the bread cubes in a single layer on a sheet pan and drizzle with a little olive oil. Toss the bread to coat. Toast the bread for 5 to 10 minutes, tossing once or twice to brown evenly. Set aside.

4. Add the asparagus and snap peas to the boiling water and cook for 2 to 3 minutes. Drain and rinse under cold water until cool. Blanching these vegetables makes them tender and easier to chew, which will blend nicely with the other vegetable textures.

5. In a large bowl, combine the arugula, zucchini, tomatoes, red onion, asparagus, snap peas, olives, mozzarella, and toasted bread cubes. Toss to mix.

CONTINUED

6. Whisk the dressing again and add it to the salad. Toss to coat and top with the fresh basil.
7. Refrigerate leftovers in an airtight container for 2 to 3 days.

MAKE IT EASIER Use a store-bought vinaigrette rather than making your own or use purchased croutons. Pre-chopped vegetables can also be used to reduce prep time. You can also use 1 large beefsteak tomato, halved and diced, instead of cherry tomatoes.

PER SERVING (INCLUDES OPTIONAL INGREDIENTS)
Calories: 307; Total fat: 24g; Carbohydrates: 11g; Fiber: 3g; Protein: 13g; Calcium: 302mg; Vitamin D: 0mcg; Vitamin B12: 1mcg; Iron: 3mg; Zinc: 2mg

Green Riches

Salad greens contain vitamins and minerals and they provide fiber, which is essential for a healthy body. They are also low in calories yet high in nutrients, making salads an ideal food for weight management. However, not all greens are created equal. Some of the most nutritious greens include kale, spinach, romaine lettuce, and arugula. These greens are rich in vitamins A, C, and K as well as potassium and several B vitamins, including folate. By eating a salad or two a day, one can consume all of the daily vegetable requirements.

MEDITERRANEAN BEAN SALAD

SERVES 4 to 6
PREP TIME: 15 minutes
CHILL TIME: 1 hour

1 tablespoon ground cumin

1½ teaspoons dried oregano

1 (15.5-ounce) can chickpeas, drained and rinsed

1 (15.5-ounce) can cannellini beans, drained and rinsed

1 (15.5-ounce) can black beans, drained and rinsed

2 Persian cucumbers, diced small

1 red onion, diced small

½ cup Kalamata olives, sliced

1 bunch fresh dill, chopped

Juice of 1 lemon

Beans are a great source of protein, and this salad is packed full with chickpeas, cannellini beans, and black beans. But the best part is the Mediterranean flavor. The cucumbers, olives, and fresh dill pair splendidly with the cooked beans for one tasty and unique bean salad.

1. In a small bowl, stir together the cumin and oregano. Set aside.
2. In a large bowl, combine the chickpeas, cannellini beans, black beans, cucumbers, red onion, olives, and dill. Toss to incorporate thoroughly.
3. Sprinkle the spice mix and lemon juice over the salad and toss to combine. Refrigerate for 1 hour before serving.
4. Refrigerate leftovers in an airtight container for up to 4 days.

MAKE IT EASIER You can always swap black beans for dried orca beans, which will need to be cooked ahead of time. Orca beans are also known as calypso beans, yin yang, or vaquero, and are named for their black-and-white color. They have a creamy texture. If you own an Instant Pot or electric pressure cooker, this can be a great tool for cooking dried beans. Additionally, dried beans are a reasonably priced pantry item for stocking up.

PER SERVING Calories: 317; Total fat: 18g; Carbohydrates: 54g; Fiber: 16g; Protein: 4g; Calcium: 117mg; Vitamin D: 0mcg; Vitamin B12: 0mcg; Iron: 6mg; Zinc: 3mg

DANDELION AND CITRUS SALAD

SERVES 4 to 6
PREP TIME: 15 minutes

1 bunch fresh dandelion
    greens, chopped
1 medium fennel bulb, halved and
    thinly sliced
2 oranges, peeled and cut into slices
1 small radicchio, chopped
1 avocado, peeled, pitted, and diced
2 tablespoons hemp hearts
¼ cup raw, slivered almonds
Balsamic vinegar, for
    dressing (optional)

Dandelion greens are an often underutilized vegetable, but they are packed with vitamins and nutrients, especially when consumed raw. They are abundant in the springtime, so gobble them up when you can find them! The greens can be a little bitter, but in this salad, the oranges offset their sharp taste. With the creamy avocado and the anise-like flavor of fennel, you have one flavorful salad that is also protein rich, thanks to the hemp hearts and raw almonds.

1. Place the dandelion greens in a large bowl.
2. Layer on the fennel, oranges, radicchio, and avocado. Top with hemp hearts and almonds.
3. Serve with the vinegar on the side, if desired.
4. Refrigerate any leftovers in an airtight container for 2 to 3 days.

SUBSTITUTION If you are weary of dandelion greens (or they're just out of season), try this salad with spinach or romaine lettuce. You will still have healthy raw greens and a salad rich in vitamin C and heart-healthy protein.

PER SERVING Calories: 237; Total fat: 15g; Carbohydrates: 21g; Fiber: 9g; Protein: 9g; Calcium: 178mg; Vitamin D: 0mcg; Vitamin B12: 0mcg; Iron: 4mg; Zinc: 2mg

ROMANESCO AND CHICKPEA SALAD

SERVES 6
PREP TIME: 15 minutes
COOK TIME: 5 minutes

1 large head Romanesco, cut into
    bite-size chunks

¼ cup olive oil

2 tablespoons red wine vinegar

2 tablespoons horseradish mustard

Juice of 1 lemon

1 (15.5-ounce) can chickpeas, drained
    and rinsed

4 radishes, trimmed, halved, and
    thinly sliced

2 small shallots, halved and thinly sliced

1 small bunch fresh mint, leaves
    finely chopped

¼ cup raisins

¼ cup sunflower seeds

If you are unfamiliar with Romanesco, it will remind you of cauliflower or broccoli but it is neither. When blanched, it has a slight crunch. The creamy horseradish vinaigrette adds a zesty finish to this salad.

1. Bring a large pot of water to boil over high heat. In a large bowl, place several ice cubes and fill the bowl with cold water.

2. Add the Romanesco to the boiling water and blanch for 3 minutes. Drain and immediately plunge it into the ice water to cool. Work in batches if necessary. Drain the Romanesco after it cools.

3. In a small bowl, whisk the olive oil, vinegar, mustard, and lemon juice until well incorporated. Set aside.

4. In another large bowl, combine the chickpeas, radishes, shallots, cooled Romanesco, mint, raisins, and sunflower seeds. Toss to incorporate.

5. Drizzle a small amount of the dressing on the salad and toss again to coat. Serve in bowls with extra dressing on the side, if desired.

6. Refrigerate leftovers in an airtight container for 3 to 4 days.

SUBSTITUTION Use broccoli or cauliflower for the Romanesco. If you don't love horseradish, the dressing can be replaced with a red wine vinaigrette or something similar that's store-bought.

PER SERVING Calories: 239; Total fat: 14g; Carbohydrates: 25g; Fiber: 7g; Protein: 8g; Calcium: 78mg; Vitamin D: 0mcg; Vitamin B12: 0mcg; Iron: 3mg; Zinc: 1mg

PEACH AND PEPITA SLAW

SERVES 8
PREP TIME: 15 minutes

1 tablespoon rice vinegar or apple
  cider vinegar
1 tablespoon mirin or sweet white wine
1 tablespoon grated, peeled
  fresh ginger
1½ teaspoons miso paste
1 head radicchio, halved and very
  thinly sliced
1 small head green cabbage, halved
  and very thinly sliced
2 peaches, halved, pitted, and cut
  into matchsticks
3 small kohlrabi, grated on the large
  holes of a box grater
3 scallions, thinly sliced
1 bunch fresh mint, chopped, plus
  leaves for garnish (optional)
2 tablespoons pepitas, plus more for
  garnish (optional)

This fresh seasonal coleslaw is a great way to enjoy peaches, even if they are a little under-ripe. Cut into matchstick-size pieces, they provide sweetness in each bite along with hearty cabbage, kohlrabi, and radicchio. Fresh mint pairs splendidly with the miso-ginger dressing, and pepitas add a nice crunch.

1. In a small bowl, whisk the vinegar, mirin, ginger, and miso to combine.
2. Separate the radicchio and cabbage slices into shavings with your fingers and transfer to a large bowl.
3. Add the peaches, kohlrabi, scallions, mint, and pepitas. Stir to combine.
4. Pour the dressing over the slaw and stir until coated.
5. Garnish with extra mint and pepitas before serving, if desired.
6. Refrigerate leftovers in an airtight container for 3 to 4 days.

MAKE IT EASIER Store-bought chopped coleslaw mix can also be used to reduce the preparation time, or use a mandoline or the pulse option on a food processor to shred the kohlrabi, radicchio, and cabbage quickly.

PER SERVING Calories: 63; Total fat: 0g; Carbohydrates: 14g; Fiber: 5g; Protein: 3g; Calcium: 59mg; Vitamin D: 0mcg; Vitamin B12: 0mcg; Iron: 1mg; Zinc: 0mg

SPICY AVOCADO GAZPACHO

SERVES 8
PREP TIME: 20 minutes
CHILL TIME: 2 hours

12 tomatillos, husked, rinsed well,
   and halved
2 avocados, pitted and peeled
2 garlic cloves, peeled
1 English cucumber, quartered
   and seeded
1 jalapeño pepper, halved and seeded,
   plus slices for garnish
Juice of 1 lime
1 bunch fresh basil leaves, plus more
   for garnish
¼ cup almond milk, plus more
   as needed
2 tablespoons olive oil
½ teaspoon red pepper
   flakes (optional)
Salt
Freshly ground black pepper

This slightly different take on gazpacho is full of healthy green veggies, creamy avocado, and just the right amount of heat thanks to the jalapeño. Tomatillos are a great alternative to traditional tomatoes, and they give the soup a beautiful green hue. This chilled soup is perfect on a hot day as a full meal or light appetizer, depending on serving size. It's also great for events or gatherings because it can easily be made in advance. Serve it in small cups or even in shot glasses for an amuse-bouche.

1. In a high-speed blender, working in batches as needed, combine the tomatillos, avocados, garlic, cucumber, jalapeño, lime juice, basil, almond milk, olive oil, and red pepper flakes (if using). Season with salt and black pepper. Purée until completely blended. Add more almond milk if the soup is too thick.
2. Transfer to a large bowl and refrigerate until chilled.
3. Serve garnished with jalapeño slices and basil leaves.
4. Refrigerate leftovers in an airtight container for up to 4 days.

MIX IT UP Adjust the heat level according to your preference. A bell pepper can replace the jalapeño for a milder soup, or use a serrano for even more heat. Just don't forget the creamy avocado, as it is the star of this chilled soup.

PER SERVING Calories: 130; Total fat: 11g; Carbohydrates: 9g; Fiber: 4g; Protein: 2g; Calcium: 57mg; Vitamin D: 0mcg; Vitamin B12: 0mcg; Iron: 1mg; Zinc: 0mg

CREAMY WILD RICE SOUP

SERVES 4
PREP TIME: 1 hour
COOK TIME: 25 minutes

4 tablespoons butter

1 onion, diced

1 celery stalk, diced

1 carrot, diced

2 tablespoons fresh thyme leaves

3 tablespoons flour of choice

3 cups vegetable broth

1½ cups wild rice, cooked according to the package directions

½ cup dried cranberries

1 cup milk

Salt

Freshly ground black pepper

Wild rice is a staple in Minnesota, and it shines in this regional specialty. It's extra-creamy and rich from the addition of milk and butter. But the best part has to be the nutty wild rice with its complexity and texture. The rice is cooked before making the soup. Wild rice takes much longer to cook than other varieties, so it can even be made in advance and refrigerated until ready to use. Once the wild rice is cooked, the rest of the soup comes together quickly and easily. Enjoy this lovely soup with bread or crackers.

1. In a stockpot over medium heat, melt the butter. Add the onion, celery, carrot, and thyme. Sauté for 2 to 3 minutes.

2. Stir in the flour until smooth.

3. While stirring, gradually add the vegetable broth until incorporated. Increase the heat to medium-high. Cook, stirring constantly, until the soup becomes thicker, about 5 minutes.

4. Stir in the wild rice and cranberries. Reduce the heat to low. Simmer the soup for 10 minutes.

5. Stir in the milk. Taste and season with salt and pepper. Serve immediately.

6. Refrigerate any leftovers in an airtight container for up to 4 days.

ANIMAL STYLE If family members prefer meat, shredded chicken can be added to this rich and creamy soup. Roast the chicken separately and add it just before serving in individual bowls.

PER SERVING Calories: 462; Total fat: 14g; Carbohydrates: 76g; Fiber: 6g; Protein: 12g; Calcium: 106mg; Vitamin D: 8mcg; Vitamin B12: 0mcg; Iron: 2mg; Zinc: 2mg

KABOCHA SQUASH AND HERB SOUP

SERVES 6
PREP TIME: 15 minutes
COOK TIME: 35 minutes

2 tablespoons olive oil, divided

1 small kabocha squash, peeled, seeded, and cubed

1 tablespoon butter

4 garlic cloves, minced

1 large onion, chopped

2 tomatoes, seeded and chopped

3 large Swiss chard leaves, stems separated, leaves and stems chopped

5 rosemary sprigs

5 thyme sprigs

Salt

Freshly ground black pepper

2½ cups vegetable broth

¾ cup coconut milk

SUBSTITUTION The kabocha can be replaced with another squash such as butternut, delicata, or acorn. Additionally, pumpkin is a terrific substitution. If you are short on time, frozen cubed butternut squash (two 12-ounce bags) works great as well

Kabocha squash is also known as Japanese pumpkin. It has a sweet and creamy flesh that's terrific for soup. In this version, it's roasted, cut into bite-size pieces, and added to a savory vegetable herb broth. The squash fills you up, and the broth is soul-warming. Just don't skimp on the fresh herbs. Fresh rosemary and thyme bring this soup to the next level. Fall eating doesn't get any better than this soup.

1. Preheat the oven to 375° F. Coat a baking sheet with 1 tablespoon of olive oil.
2. On the prepared baking sheet, arrange the kabocha squash in a single layer.
3. Bake for 15 to 20 minutes, or until the squash is slightly browned and soft. Set aside.
4. In a large stockpot over medium heat, heat the remaining 1 tablespoon of olive oil and melt the butter. Add the garlic, onion, tomatoes, Swiss chard stems, rosemary, and thyme. Season with salt and pepper. Cook for 10 minutes, or until the onion and tomato begin to cook down.
5. Add the roasted squash, Swiss chard leaves, and vegetable broth. Bring the soup to a boil.
6. Stir in the coconut milk and remove the soup from the heat before serving.
7. Refrigerate leftovers in an airtight container for up to 4 days.

PER SERVING Calories: 154; Total fat: 13g; Carbohydrates: 10g; Fiber: 4g; Protein: 2g; Calcium: 38mg; Vitamin D: 1mcg; Vitamin B12: 0mcg; Iron: 2mg; Zinc: 0mg

PASTA FAGIOLI

SERVES 6
PREP TIME: 10 minutes
COOK TIME: 35 minutes

1 tablespoon olive oil

1 large onion, diced

2 celery stalks, chopped

3 garlic cloves, minced

Red pepper flakes, for seasoning

½ teaspoon Italian seasoning

1 (28-ounce) can crushed tomatoes

2 (15.5-ounce) cans cannellini beans, drained and rinsed

4 cups vegetable broth

1 Parmesan cheese rind (optional)

8 ounces elbow pasta, cooked until al dente and drained

¼ cup pesto (optional)

𝒫asta fagioli is a traditional Italian soup whose name means "pasta and beans." This soup is hearty yet inexpensive to make. Cannellini beans are typically used, but any bean variety will work. If you have a Parmesan rind handy, it provides extra flavor when simmered in this soup. Just be sure to remove the rind before serving. The cheese department of any grocery store will often sell rinds at minimal cost or give them out free—just ask. Basil pesto tastes great as a garnish along with lots of freshly grated Parmesan, as you like.

1. In a large stockpot over medium heat, heat the olive oil. Add the onion, celery, and garlic. Sauté for about 3 minutes until the onion is fragrant and translucent.

2. Season with the red pepper flakes and stir in the Italian seasoning and tomatoes. Bring the soup to a simmer, stirring occasionally.

3. Add the beans, vegetable broth, and rind (if using). Return the soup to a simmer and cook, stirring occasionally, for 15 to 20 minutes.

4. Stir in the pasta and simmer for 2 to 3 minutes to warm. Discard the rind and serve the soup garnished with pesto (if using).

5. Refrigerate leftovers in an airtight container for up to 5 days.

MIX IT UP Replace the elbow macaroni with ditalini pasta, which is a very short cylindrical pasta used in traditional Italian Pasta Fagioli. However, you could also use orzo or rice for a change from the traditional.

PER SERVING Calories: 342; Total fat: 4g; Carbohydrates: 64g; Fiber: 13g; Protein: 16g; Calcium: 99mg; Vitamin D: 0mcg; Vitamin B12: 0mcg; Iron: 6mg; Zinc: 1mg

ACORN MISO RAMEN

SERVES 4
PREP TIME: 15 minutes
COOK TIME: 25 minutes

2 tablespoons olive oil, divided

1 acorn squash, halved, seeded, and
    cut into thin slices

2 lemons, halved

2 red onions, very thinly sliced

1 cup oyster mushrooms, left whole or
    roughly chopped

4 scallions, sliced and divided

3 tablespoons white miso paste

2 tablespoons chili sauce

4 cups vegetable broth

1 (3-ounce) package ramen noodles
    (dried or fresh)

Miso is a traditional Japanese flavoring made by fermenting soybeans with salt. It is a paste-like substance commonly used to make miso soup, but it adds tremendous flavor to anything and everything. In this soup, it adds depth to the savory mushroom broth and the acorn squash brings sweetness. It's salty, sweet, and just plain delicious.

1. Preheat the oven to 400° F. Coat a baking sheet with 1 tablespoon of olive oil. Place the squash slices and lemon halves on the prepared baking sheet.

2. Bake for 15 to 20 minutes, flipping the squash halfway through the cooking time.

3. While the squash bakes, in a deep-sided skillet over medium-high heat, combine the remaining 1 tablespoon of olive oil and red onions. Cook for about 15 minutes, stirring frequently, until the onions caramelize. Add the mushrooms and half of the scallions. Cook for 2 minutes, stirring frequently.

4. Stir in the miso paste and chili sauce until thoroughly combined. Add the vegetable broth. Let the mixture come to a simmer, stirring occasionally.

5. Add the ramen noodles. Cook for 4 minutes, until the noodles soften.

6. Divide the ramen among 4 bowls. Top with the squash slices and 1 lemon half each, for squeezing. Garnish with the remaining scallions.

CONTINUED

7. Refrigerate any leftover soup in an airtight container for up to 3 days. Store the squash separately and add it to anything from salads to tacos.

MIX IT UP Acorn squash isn't the only option for this tasty ramen. Give delicata, honeynut, summer, or butternut squash a try, or even pumpkin or kabocha. Experiment to find your personal favorite.

PER SERVING Calories: 228; Total fat: 10g; Carbohydrates: 36g; Fiber: 5g; Protein: 6g; Calcium: 68mg; Vitamin D: 5mcg; Vitamin B12: 0mcg; Iron: 3mg; Zinc: 0mg

The First Vegetarians

The word *vegetarian* is actually a relatively new word. It began being used in the nineteenth century. Before that, people used the word *Pythagorean* to refer to a meatless diet, after the Greek mathematician and astronomer Pythagoras. Pythagoras followed a meat-free diet because he believed humans were reincarnated as animals, and he thought slaughtering and eating an animal was inhumane.

Chapter Six

Sandwiches and Wraps

BUTTER BEAN AND MUSHROOM TARTINE

SERVES 4
PREP TIME: 15 minutes
COOK TIME: 20 minutes

1 large loaf sourdough bread, cut into
    ½-inch-thick slices
2 tablespoons olive oil, divided
3 garlic cloves (2 cloves minced; 1 clove
    peeled and left whole)
1 (15-ounce) can butter beans, drained
    and rinsed
1 pint baby bella mushrooms, sliced
Grated Parmesan cheese, for
    garnish (optional)
Microgreens, or fresh basil leaves, for
    garnish (optional)

SUBSTITUTION Instead of butter beans, use another bean like cannellini beans or mashed chickpeas. To make prep even easier, a premade hummus could replace the mashed beans.

Tartines are open-face sandwiches, originating in France. The word means "toast." In this recipe the mashed butter beans provide creamy protein, and the sautéed mushrooms and garlic bring incredible flavor that is on full display. Top with grated Parmesan and microgreens or fresh basil for one beautiful sandwich.

1. Preheat the oven to 350° F. Line a baking sheet with parchment paper. Arrange the bread slices on the prepared baking sheet.
2. Bake the bread for 5 minutes. Flip the slices over and bake for 5 minutes, or until the slices are golden brown.
3. In a skillet over medium heat, heat 1 tablespoon of olive oil. Add the 2 minced garlic cloves and butter beans, and sauté for 3 to 4 minutes. Transfer the beans to a bowl and partially mash them with a fork. (If the bean mash seems dry, add a splash of milk for creaminess.) Set aside.
4. Return the skillet to the heat and add the remaining 1 tablespoon of olive oil. Add the mushrooms and sauté about 5 minutes, until they are lightly browned.
5. Rub each piece of toasted bread with the remaining whole garlic clove. This adds lots of flavor, but it is optional if you are garlic-shy.
6. Spread the mashed beans on each piece of garlic toast and top each with the mushroom mixture.
7. Garnish with Parmesan (if using) and microgreens (if using).

PER SERVING Calories: 411; Total fat: 9g; Carbohydrates: 68g; Fiber: 8g; Protein: 16g; Calcium: 20mg; Vitamin D: 5mcg; Vitamin B12: 1mcg; Iron: 5mg; Zinc: 1mg

BRIE WRAP with RASPBERRY VINAIGRETTE

SERVES 2
PREP TIME: 15 minutes

10 fresh or frozen and
    thawed raspberries
½ cup olive oil
¼ cup red wine vinegar
1 tablespoon dried basil
2 whole-wheat tortilla wraps
½ (6-ounce) wheel Brie cheese, cut into
    ¼-inch-thick slices
2 Swiss chard leaves, loosely chopped
8 cherry tomatoes, halved
½ Persian cucumber, thinly sliced
¼ cup currants or raisins

This simple wrap is creamy, fresh, and has just the right amount of sweetness. Homemade raspberry vinaigrette gives it that special touch, but store-bought dressing may be used to save time. Feel free to replace the Swiss chard with any lettuce, which will provide a nice healthy crunch to this sandwich.

1. In a blender or food processor, combine the raspberries, olive oil, vinegar, and basil. Purée until blended completely and smooth. Set aside.
2. Place the tortillas on a work surface. Evenly divide the Brie, Swiss chard, tomatoes, cucumber, and currants among the tortillas, placing the ingredients in the center of each.
3. Drizzle the filling with the vinaigrette.
4. Wrap the tortilla around the filling and fold in the bottom tightly to keep the filling in.

ANIMAL STYLE Any deli or prepared meat can be added to this wrap. The meat will not need a lot of seasoning due to the rich Brie and tart vinaigrette.

PER SERVING Calories: 1,098; Total fat: 80g; Carbohydrates: 75g; Fiber: 18g; Protein: 31g; Calcium: 267mg; Vitamin D: 0mcg; Vitamin B12: 2mcg; Iron: 4mg; Zinc: 3mg

COLLARD GREEN BREAKFAST BURRITO

SERVES 4
PREP TIME: 15 minutes
COOK TIME: 30 minutes

2 tablespoons olive oil, divided

1 butternut squash, peeled and diced

1 onion, diced

2 garlic cloves, minced

1 bunch collard greens, stemmed
  and chopped

4 large eggs

Salt

Freshly ground black pepper

4 flour tortillas

½ cup shredded Cheddar
  cheese (optional)

½ cup salsa (optional)

Collard greens are a Southern staple and with good reason. They are a good source of vitamins A and K, which help support strong bones. This tasty breakfast burrito is filled with greens, butternut squash, and scrambled eggs. Even better, the burritos can be made in advance and frozen for a quick and easy breakfast later on. To reheat, wrap a paper towel around the burrito and microwave it for a filling breakfast that can be taken on the run.

1. Preheat the oven to 400° F. Coat a baking sheet with 1 tablespoon of olive oil. Arrange the squash on the prepared baking sheet in a single layer.

2. Roast for 25 to 30 minutes, flipping halfway through the cooking time. The cooked squash should be soft and lightly browned.

3. In a skillet over medium-low heat, add the remaining 1 tablespoon of olive oil, the onion, and garlic. Sauté for 1 to 2 minutes, stirring constantly, until the onion is fragrant.

4. Add the collard greens to the skillet. Cook for 1 to 2 minutes, stirring constantly, until they wilt. Remove from the heat and set aside.

5. In a medium bowl, whisk the eggs. Season with salt and pepper and whisk again to combine.

CONTINUED

COLLARD GREEN BREAKFAST BURRITO
CONTINUED

6. In another skillet over medium heat, cook the eggs for 4 to 5 minutes, stirring constantly, until firm and lightly browned, or cook to the desired consistency. Spoon some of the eggs into the center of each tortilla and top with the wilted collard greens and roasted squash. Add cheese (if using) and salsa (if using) and wrap the burrito. Serve immediately.

7. Refrigerate leftovers in an airtight container for 2 to 3 days.

MIX IT UP If you want a lower-carb option, rather than using a traditional tortilla, use a collard green as your wrap. Simply steam the green, fill, and roll as you would for a burrito.

PER SERVING Calories: 362; Total fat: 16g; Carbohydrates: 46g; Fiber: 6g; Protein: 13g; Calcium: 209mg; Vitamin D: 18mcg; Vitamin B12: 1mcg; Iron: 4mg; Zinc: 1mg

CHICKPEA FRITTER SANDWICH

SERVES 6
PREP TIME: 15 minutes
RESTING TIME: 1 hour
COOK TIME: 30 minutes

1 tablespoon olive oil
3 cups water
2 cups chickpea flour
¼ teaspoon salt
¼ teaspoon freshly ground
   black pepper
6 hamburger buns
8 ounces ricotta
1 cup shredded Parmesan cheese
1 bunch fresh basil leaves

MIX IT UP If you would like to forego the bun for a carb-free meal, use the chickpea fritter as a topping for any salad or serve the fritter over rice or another grain.

Chickpeas are a healthy plant-based protein that make a great meat replacer. In this fritter sandwich, chickpea flour (we like Bob's Red Mill, available at most grocery stores) is mixed into a batter and baked into a small patty. This traditional Sicilian chickpea sandwich is referred to as a panelle special, and it is special indeed.

1. Coat a baking sheet with the olive oil.
2. In a saucepan, whisk the water, flour, salt, and pepper until well combined and smooth. Place the pan over medium-high heat and cook for 1 to 2 minutes, whisking constantly, until the liquid becomes a thick batter. Quickly spread the batter into an even thin layer, about ¼ inch thick, on the prepared baking sheet. Set aside to cool for at least 1 hour.
3. Preheat the oven to 400° F.
4. When the fritter is cool, slice it into 3-inch squares, or other desired shape. Separate the squares on the baking sheet pan to give each piece space. Use two sheets, if necessary.
5. Bake the fritters for 25 minutes, flipping halfway through the baking time for even browning.
6. If desired, turn the oven to broil and toast the inside of the buns, watching closely until browned.
7. Place 2 or 3 pieces of fritter on each bun and top with a large spoonful of ricotta. Garnish with Parmesan and basil before adding the top bun.

PER SERVING Calories: 372; Total fat: 13g; Carbohydrates: 42g; Fiber: 4g; Protein: 22g; Calcium: 352mg; Vitamin D: 0mcg; Vitamin B12: 2mcg; Iron: 3mg; Zinc: 2mg

TEMPEH SLOPPY JOE

SERVES 6
PREP TIME: 15 minutes
COOK TIME: 20 minutes

1 cup daikon, or radish, julienned
1 cup thinly sliced red cabbage
1 tablespoon apple cider vinegar, or
   white vinegar
1 tablespoon olive oil
1 onion, diced
2 garlic cloves, minced
1 green bell pepper, diced
1 (8-ounce) package tempeh, crumbled
1 cup dried red lentils
2 cups water
1 cup barbecue sauce
6 brioche buns, or hamburger buns
Leaves from 1 bunch fresh cilantro

Sloppy joe sandwiches are classic Americana. They are easy, filling, and tasty. In this meat-free version, crumbled tempeh and lentils replace the ground beef. However, the barbecue sauce and seasoning remain, making this vegetarian sandwich pure comfort food your whole family will enjoy. Serve the Sloppy Joe on small slider buns or regular buns topped with the cabbage and daikon slaw.

1. In a medium bowl, stir together the daikon, cabbage, and vinegar. Set aside.
2. In a stockpot over medium-high heat, combine the olive oil, onion, and garlic. Sauté for 2 to 3 minutes, stirring frequently. Add the green bell pepper and tempeh, and cook for 4 minutes.
3. Reduce the heat to low and stir in the lentils and water. Cover the pot and cook for 5 to 7 minutes, or until the lentils are tender. Uncover the pot and raise the heat to medium. Cook for about 3 minutes, stirring, until the excess water evaporates.
4. Stir in the barbecue sauce. Cook for 1 minute to warm, and remove from the heat. Serve on rolls and top with the slaw and cilantro.
5. Refrigerate any leftover filling in an airtight container for up to 5 days.

MAKE IT EASIER This is a terrific recipe to make in an Instant Pot or other electric pressure cooker to save time. It can also be made in a slow cooker. Simply put all the ingredients in and cook for 10 minutes in the pressure cooker at high pressure, or 3 hours on high heat in a slow cooker.

PER SERVING Calories: 408; Total fat: 9g; Carbohydrates: 64g; Fiber: 12g; Protein: 20g; Calcium: 143mg; Vitamin D: 0mcg; Vitamin B12: 0mcg; Iron: 5mg; Zinc: 3mg

EGGPLANT CAPONATA SANDWICH

SERVES 6
PREP TIME: 15 minutes
COOK TIME: 40 minutes

1 large eggplant, cut into 1-inch cubes
2 tablespoons olive oil, divided
1 onion, coarsely chopped
4 garlic cloves, minced
1 red bell pepper, coarsely chopped
1 large beefsteak tomato,
   coarsely chopped
1¼ cups water, divided
2 tablespoons tomato paste
5 tablespoons red wine vinegar
3 tablespoons capers
1 cup mixed pitted olives
½ teaspoon dried basil
1 (8-ounce) ball fresh mozzarella
   cheese, cut into ¼-inch-thick slices
   or slightly thicker
1 large loaf Italian bread, halved
   lengthwise and cut crosswise into
   6 pieces
Balsamic vinegar, for drizzling (optional)

This sandwich is worth the effort. Caponata is a sweet and savory spread of roasted eggplant, tomato, bell pepper, olives, and capers. It's delicious on its own, served as a side, or as a dressing for a sandwich like this one. Be sure to buy fresh mozzarella and crusty Italian bread for this. The flavors of the caponata will taste even better when paired with the cheese and crunchy bread. Even better, you will have leftover caponata for an easy appetizer or pasta topping for later.

1. Preheat the oven to 400° F.
2. Spread the eggplant evenly on a baking sheet. Drizzle with 1 tablespoon of olive oil. Roast for about 15 minutes, or until the eggplant is soft. Remove and let cool.
3. In a deep skillet over medium heat, heat the remaining 1 tablespoon of olive oil. Add the onion and cook for about 5 minutes, or until aromatic and slightly translucent. Add the garlic and cook for 5 minutes.
4. Add the red bell pepper and cook for 5 to 6 minutes to soften. If you notice the pan getting dry, add ¼ cup water. Add the tomato and simmer for 4 to 5 minutes, until it begins to cook down and looks almost like a stew.
5. Stir in the roasted eggplant, tomato paste, and 1 cup water. Simmer for 3 to 4 minutes, or until some of the liquid has evaporated. Stir in the red wine vinegar, capers, olives, and basil.

6. Layer the mozzarella on the bread and top with the caponata. Drizzle with balsamic vinegar, if desired, before serving.

7. Refrigerate leftover caponata in an airtight container for up to 5 days.

MAKE IT EASIER Make the eggplant caponata on the weekend so it is ready for quick sandwiches during the week. It stores incredibly well and even begins to taste better after the flavors have had a chance to meld.

PER SERVING Calories: 345; Total fat: 18g; Carbohydrates: 33g; Fiber: 6g; Protein: 15g; Calcium: 280mg; Vitamin D: 0mcg; Vitamin B12: 1mcg; Iron: 3mg; Zinc: 2mg

LEMON PESTO GRILLED CHEESE

SERVES 4
PREP TIME: 20 minutes
COOK TIME: 5 minutes

½ lemon, thinly sliced

2 tablespoons sugar

¼ teaspoon salt

1 bunch fresh dill, stemmed

4 garlic cloves, peeled

¼ cup grated Parmesan cheese

¼ cup olive oil

3 tablespoons butter

8 slices sandwich bread

8 slices Fontina cheese, or mild
   provolone, Gruyère, or Gouda

MIX IT UP To please the children in your household, omit the dill pesto and preserved lemon. Fontina cheese makes a delicious grilled cheese sandwich that everyone will enjoy.

Grilled cheese is the ultimate comfort food and this one is satisfying as well as scrumptious. Not only is there velvety, melty Fontina cheese but also aromatic preserved lemon and bright dill pesto. Sourdough bread delivers a light and fluffy texture, but any bread will work. This is not your kid's grilled cheese. It can be served alongside a cup of your favorite soup or with a side salad for a meal sure to delight your adult palate.

1. In a small bowl, combine the lemon slices, sugar, and salt. Stir to coat. Set aside for at least 10 minutes, stirring periodically.

2. In a food processor, combine the dill, garlic, and Parmesan cheese. Blend on low speed while slowly drizzling the olive oil into the mixture. Blend until smooth and emulsified. Transfer the pesto to a small bowl and set aside.

3. Butter each slice of bread on one side.

4. On the non-buttered side of each slice, place 2 cheese slices. Add a layer of the pesto and a few slices of preserved lemon. Close the sandwiches with the buttered-side up.

5. In a skillet over medium heat, cook the sandwiches for 1 to 2 minutes per side, or until nicely toasted. Serve immediately.

6. Store any remaining pesto in an airtight container in the refrigerator for up to one week. It can also be used on pasta, salads, or for sandwiches/wraps.

PER SERVING Calories: 576; Total fat: 41g; Carbohydrates: 31g; Fiber: 2g; Protein: 22g; Calcium: 544mg; Vitamin D: 6mcg; Vitamin B12: 1mcg; Iron: 2mg; Zinc: 3mg

BARBECUE SWEET POTATO SANDWICH

SERVES 4
PREP TIME: 15 minutes
COOK TIME: 15 minutes

1 tablespoon olive oil

3 cups shredded, peeled sweet potato

1 red onion, chopped in thin wedges

1 jalapeño pepper, seeded
    and chopped

½ cup barbecue sauce

4 hamburger buns, or rolls

½ cup shredded red cabbage

3 cilantro sprigs, stemmed

Sweet potatoes are rich in vitamins, minerals, antioxidants, and fiber. The fiber and antioxidants are beneficial to gut health. Potatoes promote the growth of good gut bacteria that contribute to healthy digestion and maximum nutrient absorption. They are also a good source of beta-carotene, which supports healthy vision. In this sandwich, the sweet potato is shredded to mimic a traditional pulled pork sandwich, then topped with shredded red cabbage for a nice crunch.

1. In a large, deep skillet over medium-high heat, heat the olive oil. Add the sweet potato, red onion, and jalapeño. Cook for about 5 minutes, stirring frequently, until the onion is translucent and the sweet potato is slightly browned.

2. Stir in the barbecue sauce until thoroughly combined. Reduce the heat to low and cook for 10 to 12 minutes, stirring occasionally. Remove the skillet from the heat and scoop about ½ cup of the sweet potato mixture onto each sliced bun. Top each with shredded red cabbage and cilantro. Serve warm.

3. Refrigerate any leftover filling in an airtight container for up to 5 days.

MAKE IT EASIER We recommend a mandoline for shredding the sweet potato, or using the grating blade of a food processor. A julienne peeler or cheese grater can also be used, but it will just take a little longer.

PER SERVING Calories: 297; Total fat: 6g; Carbohydrates: 56g; Fiber: 5g; Protein: 6g; Calcium: 104mg; Vitamin D: 0mcg; Vitamin B12: 0mcg; Iron: 2mg; Zinc: 0mg

PORTOBELLO AND BRIE FRENCH DIP

SERVES 4
PREP TIME: 10 minutes
COOK TIME: 35 minutes

2 tablespoons olive oil, divided
1 onion, thinly sliced
2 garlic cloves, minced
3 portobello mushrooms, thinly sliced
1 cup vegetable broth
1 tablespoon soy sauce
1 tablespoon vegetarian
   Worcestershire sauce
4 mini French baguettes or Italian
   bread, split horizontally
1 (8-ounce) wheel Brie cheese,
   thinly sliced

The French dip is a hot sandwich traditionally made of thinly sliced beef layered on a French roll that is dipped into a flavorful sauce made from the juices of the cooked meat. Two different Los Angeles restaurants claim to be the birthplace of this popular sandwich, created in the early-twentieth century. Whatever its origin, this flavorful sandwich can't be missed. In this meatless version, thinly cut portobello mushrooms replace the beef and melted Brie cheese adds decadence and creaminess. Serve alongside a small dish of the cooking liquid (au jus) for dipping.

1. In a stockpot over medium-low heat, heat 1 tablespoon of olive oil to coat the bottom of the pot. Add the onion and cook for 20 to 25 minutes, stirring occasionally, until it begins to caramelize.

2. Add the garlic and cook for 1 to 2 minutes. Transfer to a plate and set aside.

3. Return the stockpot to the stovetop and increase the heat to medium-high. Add the remaining 1 tablespoon of olive oil and the mushrooms. Cook for 8 to 10 minutes, stirring occasionally so they cook evenly, until lightly browned.

4. Return the onion and garlic mixture to the pot. Add the vegetable broth, soy sauce, and Worcestershire sauce. Bring the mixture to a low simmer and cook for 4 to 5 minutes, or until the liquid has decreased by about half. Remove from the heat.

5. Preheat the broiler.

CONTINUED

6. Place the split baguettes on a baking sheet. Line one side of the baguettes with cheese and the other side with mushrooms. Place the sheet with the open-faced sandwiches under the broiler for 1 to 2 minutes, or until the cheese begins to melt. Remove and press the halves of each sandwich together.

7. Pour the cooking liquid (au jus) into small bowls and serve with the sandwiches for dipping.

MIX IT UP To adapt this meal for a gluten-free diet, omit the bread and simply put the cooked mushrooms and cheese over fresh greens with a little drizzle of the au jus, or serve over a grain for a hearty bowl.

PER SERVING Calories: 316; Total fat: 23g; Carbohydrates: 14g; Fiber: 2g; Protein: 16g; Calcium: 116mg; Vitamin D: 3mcg; Vitamin B12: 2mcg; Iron: 1mg; Zinc: 2mg

Protein Power

It's incredibly easy for vegetarians to meet their daily protein needs with plant-based proteins such as tofu, tempeh, beans, and lentils. These meat replacements are easy to prepare and completely satisfying.

BUFFALO CAULIFLOWER WRAPS

SERVES 4
PREP TIME: 15 minutes
COOK TIME: 30 minutes

1 cup water

1 cup milk of choice

1 cup flour of choice

1 teaspoon paprika

Salt

Freshly ground black pepper

1 large head cauliflower, cored and cut
   into bite-size florets

5 tablespoons plus 1 teaspoon butter

½ cup hot sauce

4 flour tortillas

2 carrots, julienned or very thinly sliced

8 ounces chopped lettuce, any variety
   (half of a 16-ounce bag)

ANIMAL STYLE Add shredded chicken or
sliced chicken breast to the wraps with
the buffalo cauliflower for the meat
eaters in your household. Also try
some extra sauce and blue cheese
dressing on the wraps for extra flavor.

*The zesty cauliflower for this spicy wrap is prepared
by roasting it. It is then put in a wrap with fresh lettuce
and julienned carrots for a slight crunch. However, if you
prefer, you can roast the cauliflower as directed and then
use it for other dishes, such as serving alone as a hot and
spicy appetizer, over rice, or alongside macaroni and
cheese for a little extra flair. However you serve this cauliflower, it is sure to please.*

1. Preheat the oven to 400° F. Line a baking sheet with
parchment paper. Set aside.
2. In a large bowl, whisk the water, milk, flour, and
paprika until smooth. Season with salt and pepper, and
whisk again to combine.
3. Using tongs, dip each cauliflower floret in the batter
to coat and place it on the prepared baking sheet.
4. Bake for 20 minutes, flipping the florets after
10 minutes. The florets will be golden brown
when done.
5. Meanwhile, in a saucepan over medium heat, combine the butter and hot sauce. Cook, stirring, until the
butter melts. Remove from the heat.
6. Using tongs, carefully dip each floret into the sauce
and place it back onto the baking sheet. Bake for
10 minutes.
7. In a dry skillet over medium heat, warm each tortilla for 1 to 2 minutes until pliable.
8. Add the carrot, buffalo cauliflower, and lettuce to
each tortilla. Wrap and enjoy.

PER SERVING Calories: 415; Total fat: 20g; Carbohydrates: 58g;
Fiber: 9g; Protein: 13g; Calcium: 183mg; Vitamin D: 35mcg;
Vitamin B12: 0mcg; Iron: 4mg; Zinc: 1mg

Mildly seasoned curried cauliflower is roasted to crispy perfection for these taco-like daikon wraps.

CURRIED CAULIFLOWER DAIKON WRAPS

SERVES 4
PREP TIME: 10 minutes
COOK TIME: 30 minutes

1 heaping tablespoon curry powder

1 teaspoon garlic powder

1 teaspoon ground turmeric

½ teaspoon ground cumin

Grated zest of 1 lemon

Juice of 1 lemon

2 tablespoons olive oil

1 large head cauliflower, cored and separated into bite-size florets

½ cup raw cashews

1 medium-large daikon, cut into very thin disks

2 scallions, sliced

MIX IT UP If your family is not a big fan of curry, season the cauliflower with your favorite dry spices. Smoked paprika works well, or even an Italian blend. Also, using pre-cut cauliflower florets can save time when you are in a hurry.

Bite-size and utensil-free, these wraps are full of flavor and can be served as an appetizer or a complete gluten-free meal. The raw cashews provide a protein crunch, and the roasted curried cauliflower brings robust flavor. Curry powder may not be everyone's go-to choice, but these veggie wraps can be a good introduction. The curry is tasty yet surprisingly mild and will not overpower the daikon and cauliflower.

1. Preheat the oven to 400° F. Line a baking sheet with parchment paper.
2. In a large bowl, stir together the curry powder, garlic powder, turmeric, cumin, lemon zest, lemon juice, and olive oil to combine completely.
3. Add the cauliflower and cashews to the spice mix and toss until the cauliflower and nuts are well coated. Spread the cauliflower and nut mixture into a single layer on the prepared baking sheet.
4. Bake for about 30 minutes, flipping the mixture halfway through the baking time, until the cauliflower is tender and beginning to brown.
5. Lay the daikon circles on a work surface. Place a small amount of the curry mixture into the center of each circle. Fold up the sides of the daikon as you would a taco and secure with a toothpick, if desired. Garnish with scallions to serve.

PER SERVING Calories: 219; Total fat: 15g; Carbohydrates: 18g; Fiber: 6g; Protein: 8g; Calcium: 60mg; Vitamin D: 0mcg; Vitamin B12: 0mcg; Iron: 2mg; Zinc: 2mg

HULI HULI SEITAN SANDWICH

SERVES 4
PREP TIME: 10 minutes
COOK TIME: 15 minutes

1 cup pineapple juice

¼ cup liquid aminos, or soy sauce

¼ cup light brown sugar

2 tablespoons apple cider vinegar

2 tablespoons ketchup

1 teaspoon vegetarian
  Worcestershire sauce

2 garlic cloves, minced

1 (2-inch) piece fresh ginger, peeled
  and grated

1 (12-ounce) package seitan, cubed

1 teaspoon olive oil

4 small Italian hero rolls

¼ cup fresh cilantro, chopped,
  for garnish

2 scallions, thinly sliced, for garnish

In this vegetarian version of Hawaiian grilled chicken, seitan replaces the chicken, and pineapple juice is added for a sweet finish to this smoky sandwich. When shopping, look for seitan that hasn't been seasoned, or prepare your own at home using vital wheat gluten.

1. In a saucepan over medium heat, stir together the pineapple juice, liquid aminos, brown sugar, vinegar, ketchup, Worcestershire sauce, garlic, and ginger. Bring to a simmer, stirring frequently, for about 2 minutes, until the ingredients dissolve. Remove from the heat and set aside.

2. In a skillet over medium-high heat, combine the seitan and olive oil. Cook, stirring frequently, for 4 to 5 minutes, until browned.

3. Pour the sauce into the skillet to coat the seitan. Simmer for 3 to 4 minutes to thicken the sauce and glaze the seitan. Spoon the seitan and a little sauce into the rolls. Garnish with cilantro and scallions.

SUBSTITUTION Replace the seitan with tofu or even chickpeas for variety. The recipe can also be adapted for other meals such as pizza, wraps, or bowls. You can't go wrong with this sweet and savory huli huli.

PER SERVING Calories: 614; Total fat: 4g; Carbohydrates: 73g; Fiber: 3g; Protein: 72g; Calcium: 180mg; Vitamin D: 0mcg; Vitamin B12: 0mcg; Iron: 8mg; Zinc: 2mg

Chapter Seven

Beans and Grains

ITALIAN-STYLE GREENS AND BEANS

SERVES 4
PREP TIME: 10 minutes
COOK TIME: 20 minutes

1 tablespoon olive oil

1 large onion, cut into slices

3 garlic cloves, minced

2 bunches escarole, chopped

2 cups vegetable broth

1 (8-ounce) package Beyond, Impossible, or Sweet Earth ground "meat"

2 (15.5-ounce) cans cannellini beans, 1 can drained, 1 can undrained

2 tablespoons soy sauce

¼ cup sliced banana peppers, or pickled jalapeño peppers, plus more for serving

½ cup grated Parmesan cheese

SUBSTITUTION Spinach can be used in place of the escarole. You can also omit the Parmesan and use nutritional yeast or vegan Parmesan for a dairy-free option.

This classic Italian recipe is traditionally made with sautéed escarole, cannellini beans, lots of garlic, and often a generous portion of sausage. This meat-free version goes from hearty side dish to complete meal with the addition of plant-based meat crumbles. But don't forget a generous amount of Parmesan and sliced banana peppers for a superb finish. Serve over rice or with bread.

1. In a stockpot over medium-low heat, heat the olive oil. Add the onion and sauté for 10 to 12 minutes, stirring frequently, or until the onion has caramelized.

2. Add the garlic, escarole, and vegetable broth. Cover the pot and let the greens wilt, about 5 minutes.

3. While the greens cook, in a skillet over medium-low heat, cook the "meat," stirring frequently, for 7 minutes, to break it up and cook evenly.

4. Uncover the greens. Add the undrained can of beans with its liquid and the drained beans to the pot. Cook, uncovered, stirring occasionally, while the meat cooks.

5. Once the meat is cooked, stir in the soy sauce. Add the ground "meat" mixture to the beans and greens and stir to incorporate. Simmer for 1 to 2 minutes to thicken slightly. Stir in the banana peppers just before serving.

6. Top with generous amounts of Parmesan cheese and more banana peppers, as desired.

7. Refrigerate leftovers in an airtight container for 3 to 4 days.

PER SERVING Calories: 422; Total fat: 10g; Carbohydrates: 55g; Fiber: 15g; Protein: 33g; Calcium: 398mg; Vitamin D: 0mcg; Vitamin B12: 0mcg; Iron: 7mg; Zinc: 3mg

TEX-MEX ZUCCHINI BOATS

SERVES 4
PREP TIME: 25 minutes
COOK TIME: 35 minutes

3 large zucchini, halved lengthwise

Salt

Freshly ground black pepper

½ cup shredded Cheddar cheese or a
  Mexican blend, divided

1 tablespoon olive oil

1 red onion, diced small

1 large red bell pepper, seeded and
  diced small

1 jalapeño pepper, seeded and
  diced small

1 (15.5-ounce) can black beans,
  drained and rinsed

1 cup fresh or frozen corn

3 tablespoons taco seasoning

1 cup cooked quinoa

MAKE IT EASIER This meal can be prepared in advance and refrigerated until ready to bake. Simply prepare the stuffed zucchini boats and cover for up to 1 day, making this a perfect recipe for an easy Monday night meal.

Stuffed zucchini is inspired by dolma (a stuffed dish), a classic Ottoman recipe. Squash or zucchini are filled with rice and sometimes meat. In this vegetarian version, quinoa replaces the traditional rice and Southwestern flavors are incorporated for a spicy Tex-Mex flavor. Serve warm with a garnish of fresh cilantro, lime wedges, or extra jalapeño slices.

1. Preheat the oven to 400° F.
2. Scoop out the middle portion and seeds of the zucchini halves to make boats. Save the scooped-out flesh. Arrange the boats, cut-side up, in a 9-by-13-inch baking dish. Season with salt, pepper, and a small amount of the cheese. Set aside.
3. In a large saucepan over medium heat, heat the olive oil. Add the red onions, red bell pepper, and jalapeño. Cook for 3 to 4 minutes, stirring occasionally, or until the onion is fragrant and the peppers begin to soften.
4. Chop the reserved zucchini into small cubes. Add it to the mixture along with the beans, corn, and taco seasoning. Cook for about 2 minutes. Add in the quinoa and cook, stirring, until the mixture is heated through.
5. Fill the boats with the vegetable and quinoa mixture and top with more cheese. Cover the dish with aluminum foil. Bake for 25 minutes. Remove from the oven and remove the foil.
6. Turn the oven to broil. Place the zucchini in to broil for 3 to 4 minutes, depending on the desired crispiness.

PER SERVING Calories: 383; Total fat: 18g; Carbohydrates: 46g; Fiber: 12g; Protein: 16g; Calcium: 175mg; Vitamin D: 2mcg; Vitamin B12: 0mcg; Iron: 3mg; Zinc: 3mg

MIXED MUSHROOM POLENTA

SERVES 2
PREP TIME: 10 minutes
COOK TIME: 15 minutes

1 tablespoon olive oil

3 cups mixed mushrooms (cremini, oyster, or other), chopped

2 garlic cloves, minced

3½ cups vegetable broth, divided

2 tablespoons fresh thyme leaves, chopped

2 tablespoons fresh sage leaves, chopped

2 tablespoons miso paste

1 cup polenta

½ teaspoon salt

½ teaspoon freshly ground black pepper

¼ cup grated Parmesan cheese, plus more for serving

Extra-rich and creamy thanks to lots of Parmesan, this polenta is topped with a combination of cremini and oyster mushrooms. Mushrooms were made for polenta. They provide a savory umami flavor and meaty texture that is a perfect match for polenta. A quick and easy meal with tons of flavor.

1. In a skillet over medium heat, heat the olive oil. Add the mushrooms and garlic. Sauté for 5 to 6 minutes, stirring occasionally, until the mushrooms begin to brown.

2. Add ½ cup of vegetable broth, the thyme, sage, and miso paste. Stir to combine. Cover the skillet and reduce the heat to low. Let the mixture simmer to create a sauce.

3. To make the polenta, in a medium saucepan over high heat, bring the remaining 3 cups of vegetable broth to a boil.

4. Stir in the polenta and reduce the heat to low. Cook, stirring constantly, for 2 to 3 minutes, or until the polenta has absorbed all the liquid. Remove the polenta from the heat and stir in the salt, black pepper, and Parmesan cheese.

5. Plate the polenta immediately and top with the mushroom mixture. Sprinkle with extra Parmesan, as desired.

ANIMAL STYLE Serve this mixed mushroom polenta alongside steak or chicken for omnivores and with a side salad for everyone. It's a tasty and filling meal that's easy to prepare on a weeknight.

PER SERVING Calories: 289; Total fat: 18g; Carbohydrates: 26g; Fiber: 4g; Protein: 12g; Calcium: 186mg; Vitamin D: 20mcg; Vitamin B12: 0mcg; Iron: 2mg; Zinc: 2mg

MEDITERRANEAN STUFFED PEPPERS

SERVES 6
PREP TIME: 10 minutes
COOK TIME: 40 minutes

2 celery stalks, finely chopped

1 red onion, finely chopped

1 zucchini, finely chopped

1 tablespoon olive oil

10 cremini mushrooms, finely chopped

1 tablespoon ground cumin

1 tablespoon garlic powder

2 teaspoons chili powder

1 cup quinoa, cooked according to the
    package directions

¼ cup Kalamata olives, pitted
    and halved

½ cup crumbled feta cheese

6 bell peppers, any color, tops
    removed and reserved, ribs and
    seeds removed

1 bunch fresh parsley (optional)

This is an inviting twist on traditional Italian stuffed peppers. Feta cheese and olives provide tangy and salty flavors. Quinoa makes this Mediterranean variation a deliciously filling and hearty meal. Top with tahini or hummus for extra flavor and creaminess, if you like.

1. Preheat the oven to 350° F.
2. In a large skillet over medium heat, sauté the celery, red onion, and zucchini in the oil for about 3 minutes, until the onion is translucent and fragrant. Stir in the mushrooms and cook for 3 minutes.
3. Stir in the cumin, garlic powder, and chili powder. Cook for 1 minute, stirring constantly. Add the cooked quinoa to the skillet and stir to combine. Stir in the olives and feta cheese.
4. In a deep oven-safe baking pan, stand the empty bell peppers on end, fitting them close together. Fill each pepper with the quinoa mixture and place the tops back on.
5. Bake for 30 minutes, or until the peppers are soft. Garnish with parsley (if using) and serve immediately.
6. Refrigerate leftovers in an airtight container for 1 to 2 days.

ANIMAL STYLE Ground beef can be added to the peppers for those in your family who desire a meal with meat.

PER SERVING Calories: 342; Total fat: 20g; Carbohydrates: 35g; Fiber: 7g; Protein: 9g; Calcium: 106mg; Vitamin D: 0mcg; Vitamin B12: 0mcg; Iron: 3mg; Zinc: 2mg

SPICY SRIRACHA LENTILS

SERVES 8
PREP TIME: 10 minutes
COOK TIME: 30 minutes

2 tablespoons olive oil
1 large onion, chopped
3 garlic cloves, minced
2 carrots, chopped
Salt
Freshly ground black pepper
2 tablespoons ground cumin
1 tablespoon ground coriander
7 cups vegetable broth, divided
½ cup sriracha (see Note)
1 pound red lentils
1 (14.5-ounce) can diced tomatoes
1 bunch fresh cilantro, stemmed

This spicy dish brings the heat and will have you coming back for more. Lentils are an easy hands-off meal that provide lots of protein with minimal effort. The sriracha can be adjusted for your taste and preference, as described in the note in step 2. Serve over rice or another grain with freshly chopped cilantro for a filling, budget-friendly meal.

1. In a stockpot over medium heat, combine the olive oil, onion, garlic, and carrots. Sauté for 5 to 7 minutes, or until the carrots begin to soften. Season with salt and pepper.

2. Add the cumin, coriander, 1 cup of vegetable broth, and the sriracha. Stir to combine and let the mixture come to a simmer. Cook for 5 minutes. (Note: To make a less spicy dish, change ½ cup sriracha to ¼ cup sriracha and ¼ cup water.)

3. Add the lentils, tomatoes, and the remaining 6 cups of vegetable broth. Bring to a boil, then reduce the heat to maintain a simmer. Cook, uncovered, for 20 to 25 minutes, stirring occasionally, until the lentils are thoroughly cooked.

4. Garnish with plenty of cilantro.

MAKE IT EASIER This recipe can also be prepared in a slow cooker for an easy, fuss-free meal. Sauté the onion, garlic, and carrots as in step 1, then transfer to a slow cooker. Add the lentils, veggie broth, sriracha, and spices. Cover and cook for 4 hours on low heat.

PER SERVING Calories: 260; Total fat: 5g; Carbohydrates: 45g; Fiber: 7g; Protein: 15g; Calcium: 51mg; Vitamin D: 0mcg; Vitamin B12: 0mcg; Iron: 5mg; Zinc: 2mg

HERB LOVER'S LENTIL SALAD

SERVES 4
PREP TIME: 30 minutes

1 cup French (Le Puy) lentils, cooked according to the package directions
1 (5-ounce) package mixed salad greens (4 to 5 cups)
1 cup microgreens
5 radishes, trimmed and thinly sliced
1 small bunch fresh chives, finely minced
1 small bunch fresh parsley, finely minced
1 small bunch fresh tarragon or basil, finely minced
Juice of 1 lemon
Salt
Freshly ground black pepper

Lentils are the key ingredient here. Not only are they full of protein to leave you feeling full, but they are also delicious. We recommend French green lentils because they keep their form after cooking and even have a slight bite to match the crispy greens, but any lentil can be used. Just be careful not to overcook them or they will become mushy. This salad comes together quickly, so it's great for a healthy quick weeknight meal.

1. In a large bowl, combine the lentils, salad greens, microgreens, radishes, chives, parsley, and tarragon. Toss to mix.
2. Drizzle the lemon juice over the salad and season with salt and pepper.

MAKE IT EASIER Ready-to-eat store-bought lentils can be used to make this meal even faster to prepare. They can either be heated or used chilled for a refreshing salad in warm weather.

PER SERVING Calories: 158; Total fat: 1g; Carbohydrates: 27g; Fiber: 5g; Protein: 12g; Calcium: 52mg; Vitamin D: 0mcg; Vitamin B12: 0mcg; Iron: 4mg; Zinc: 1mg

BAKED FALAFEL PITA SANDWICHES

SERVES 4
PREP TIME: 10 minutes
plus overnight
COOK TIME: 35 minutes

2 tablespoons olive oil, divided
1 cup dried chickpeas, soaked in water
  overnight, drained
½ onion, chopped
3 garlic cloves, chopped
½ cup packed fresh parsley
½ cup packed fresh dill
1 teaspoon ground cumin
1 teaspoon ground coriander
½ teaspoon red pepper flakes
½ teaspoon salt
½ teaspoon baking powder
2 pita breads, halved
8 ounces lettuce, roughly chopped
2 tomatoes, chopped
Sliced red onion, for serving (optional)

MAKE IT EASIER If you don't have time
to soak the chickpeas overnight,
premade falafels can be purchased in
most grocery stores. They can be
found in the freezer section and
usually require either baking
or microwaving.

This recipe bursts with flavor. Buy fresh pita bread for the falafel sandwich and fill it with lettuce, tomato, and falafel patties. Drizzle in your favorite hummus or tahini and a little hot sauce, if desired. For a lower-carb option, skip the pita and serve the falafels over lettuce and other veggies for a nutritious platter.

1. Preheat the oven to 375° F. Coat a baking sheet with 1 tablespoon of olive oil. Set aside.

2. In a food processor, combine the chickpeas, onion, garlic, parsley, dill, cumin, coriander, red pepper flakes, salt, and baking powder. Process the mixture until well combined but not overly puréed. It should have small pieces of each ingredient throughout. Carefully remove the blade. Using your hands, press about 1½ tablespoons of the mixture into a flat patty and place it on the prepared baking sheet. Repeat until you have about 12 patties. Using a pastry brush, brush the top of each patty with some of the remaining 1 tablespoon of olive oil.

3. Bake for 20 minutes. Flip the patties over and bake for 10 to 15 minutes, or until brown.

4. Carefully open each pita half into a pocket, and fill each with lettuce, tomato, red onion (if using), and falafel patties. Serve.

5. Refrigerate leftovers in an airtight container for up to 5 days. The falafels can also be frozen for up to 1 month for use later.

PER SERVING Calories: 365; Total fat: 11g; Carbohydrates: 56g; Fiber: 14g; Protein: 15g; Calcium: 105mg; Vitamin D: 0mcg; Vitamin B12: 0mcg; Iron: 6mg; Zinc: 3mg

MILLET PILAF WITH GRILLED TOFU

SERVES 4
PREP TIME: 5 minutes
COOK TIME: 25 minutes

2 cups vegetable broth
1 tablespoon butter
1 onion, diced small
2 garlic cloves, minced
1 cup millet
½ teaspoon smoked paprika
1 teaspoon olive oil
1 (15-ounce) package tofu, drained and cut into ½-inch-thick slices
Salt
Freshly ground black pepper
½ cup frozen peas
1 bunch fresh parsley

SUBSTITUTION If you aren't familiar with millet, quinoa or rice can be used in its place. The tofu can also be replaced with grilled chicken or another meat for the omnivores in your family.

Millet is a whole grain that is gluten-free and eaten around the world, though it is not common in the United States. It comes in several varieties, pearl millet being the size sold most frequently. It is a great source of fiber, magnesium, and antioxidants. Millet does take a little longer to cook than rice and quinoa, so plan accordingly. However, you won't be disappointed with using this slightly nutty whole grain in this simple pilaf.

1. In a small saucepan over low heat, warm the vegetable broth until needed.
2. In a stockpot over medium heat, melt the butter. Add the onion and garlic. Sauté for about 3 minutes, until the onion is fragrant.
3. Stir in the millet and paprika. Cook, stirring constantly, for 2 minutes.
4. Add the heated vegetable broth to the millet and stir to incorporate. Cover the pot and simmer for about 20 minutes, or until all the liquid is absorbed.
5. While the millet simmers, coat a grill pan or skillet with olive oil and place it over medium-high heat. Add the tofu slices and cook for 3 to 4 minutes, turning, until browned. Season with salt and pepper. Set aside.
6. Fluff the cooked millet with a fork and stir in the peas. Serve immediately with the tofu and a hefty sprinkle of fresh parsley.
7. Refrigerate leftovers in an airtight container for up to 3 days.

PER SERVING Calories: 354; Total fat: 12g; Carbohydrates: 46g; Fiber: 6g; Protein: 17g; Calcium: 212mg; Vitamin D: 2mcg; Vitamin B12: 0mcg; Iron: 4mg; Zinc: 2mg

QUINOA SUSHI BOWL

SERVES 2
PREP TIME: 25 minutes

1 tablespoon rice vinegar or apple
  cider vinegar
1 cup quinoa, cooked according to the
  package directions
1 carrot, julienned
1 Persian cucumber, thinly sliced
1 avocado, peeled, pitted, and
  thinly sliced
4 radishes, trimmed and julienned
1 cup cooked, shelled edamame
1 sheet nori (dried seaweed),
  thinly sliced
1 tablespoon sesame seeds
Soy sauce, for serving

As a vegetarian, you know sushi options are delicious but often limited. Sushi bowls prepared at home are an easy and versatile choice. Use what you have on hand or follow this basic combination. As long as you have a little time for chopping, the sky's the limit. It's much easier to throw all your ingredients in a bowl rather than rolling the sushi with a sushi mat. Get creative but don't forget the soy sauce.

1. In a medium bowl, stir together the vinegar and cooked quinoa.
2. For two servings, put half the ingredients in the first serving bowl, starting with a bed of quinoa. Arrange half the carrot, cucumber, avocado, radishes, and edamame on top. Finish with half the sliced nori and sesame seeds and lightly drizzle with soy sauce.
3. Prepare the second serving bowl in the same way and serve.

SUBSTITUTION Rice can be used in place of the quinoa. White, brown, or even forbidden rice all work well. Simply prepare it as directed and add all your favorite veggies for an easy sushi bowl at home.

PER SERVING Calories: 569; Total fat: 22g; Carbohydrates: 77g; Fiber: 16g; Protein: 22g; Calcium: 190mg; Vitamin D: 0mcg; Vitamin B12: 0mcg; Iron: 7mg; Zinc: 5mg

TEMPEH SKEWERS WITH MANGO RELISH

SERVES 4
PREP TIME: 20 minutes
COOK TIME: 30 minutes

FOR THE SKEWERS

1 (1-inch) piece fresh ginger, peeled
    and grated

2 teaspoons ground turmeric

½ teaspoon cayenne pepper

½ teaspoon freshly ground
    black pepper

¼ teaspoon salt

Juice of 1 lime

2 (8-ounce) packages tempeh, cut into
    1-by-3-inch rectangles

FOR THE MANGO RELISH

1 mango, diced small

1 jalapeño pepper, diced small

1 small cucumber, diced small

1 bunch fresh cilantro, leaves chopped,
    plus more for garnish

Juice of 1 lime

½ teaspoon freshly ground
    black pepper

¼ teaspoon salt

These skewers are healthy, simple, and delicious. Tempeh is high in protein, probiotics, and is incredibly versatile. When combined with turmeric, a potent anti-inflammatory and antioxidant, you get a health powerhouse. But the best part about these skewers might be the mango relish. It's sweet, bright, and has a little kick. It's all fresh veggies and fruit, so feel free to pile it on.

TO MAKE THE SKEWERS

1. Preheat the oven to 450° F. Line a baking sheet with parchment paper. Set aside.
2. To make the marinade, stir together the ginger, turmeric, cayenne, black pepper, salt, and lime juice in a small bowl.
3. Insert a skewer into each piece of tempeh, making sure to insert it by at least 1 inch all the way through.
4. Using a spoon or basting brush, coat each skewered tempeh with the turmeric marinade. Place the skewers on the prepared baking sheet.
5. Bake for 25 to 30 minutes, flipping them halfway through the baking time.

TO MAKE THE MANGO RELISH

1. While the tempeh bakes, in a large bowl, stir together the mango, jalapeño, cucumber, cilantro, lime juice, black pepper, and salt to combine. Set aside.
2. Serve the skewers with mango relish and extra cilantro as garnish.

CONTINUED

3. Refrigerate leftovers in an airtight container for up to 4 days.

MAKE IT EASIER If you are short on time or don't have access to fresh mangos, store-bought salsa can be used for the garnish. We recommend a sweeter salsa, such as a corn or pineapple salsa, if mango is not available.

PER SERVING Calories: 262; Total fat: 12g; Carbohydrates: 22g; Fiber: 1g; Protein: 22g; Calcium: 143mg; Vitamin D: 0mcg; Vitamin B12: 0mcg; Iron: 3mg; Zinc: 2mg

MISO MUSHROOMS OVER RICE

SERVES 4
PREP TIME: 20 minutes
COOK TIME: 35 minutes

1 tablespoon sesame oil or other cooking oil

6 king oyster mushrooms

4½ tablespoons white miso paste

2 tablespoons vegetable broth

2 teaspoons chili sauce

1½ teaspoons agave

1½ teaspoons liquid aminos or soy sauce

1 cup forbidden black rice or other rice, cooked according to the package directions

1 tablespoon sesame seeds

2 tablespoons chopped fresh chives

There is one kitchen staple we just can't live without— miso. This savory paste adds deep flavor to a variety of dishes, including these miso-glazed mushrooms. The sweet yet salty sauce adds a deeper layer of flavor to any dish, and you may find yourself using it in countless recipes.

1. Preheat the oven to 400° F. Coat a baking sheet with sesame oil. Set aside.
2. Halve the mushrooms lengthwise and score the cut side in a shallow crosshatch pattern. Place the mushrooms, scored-side up, on the prepared baking sheet, and bake for 15 minutes.
3. Meanwhile, in a saucepan over medium heat, whisk the miso paste, vegetable broth, chili sauce, agave, and liquid aminos to combine thoroughly. Simmer the sauce for about 5 minutes, stirring constantly, until the sauce begins to thicken.
4. Flip the mushrooms over and bake for 15 minutes more.
5. Flip the mushrooms one last time. Liberally brush them with the sauce. Cook for 5 minutes to allow the sauce to glaze the mushrooms.
6. Serve over the rice. Garnish with sesame seeds and chives.
7. Refrigerate leftovers in an airtight container for up to 3 days.

ANIMAL STYLE The miso glaze can be used over any meat. Prepare the glaze, coat, and roast any and everything. It also works great for grilling.

PER SERVING Calories: 276; Total fat: 8g; Carbohydrates: 45g; Fiber: 3g; Protein: 8g; Calcium: 63mg; Vitamin D: 0mcg; Vitamin B12: 0mcg; Iron: 2mg; Zinc: 2mg

SPICY BEAN CHILI

SERVES 6
PREP TIME: 10 minutes
COOK TIME: 25 minutes

1 tablespoon plus ¼ teaspoon olive
   oil, divided

1 large onion large, diced

3 garlic cloves, minced

1 jalapeño pepper, diced small

2 carrots, diced

¼ cup tomato paste

2 teaspoons chili powder

1 teaspoon ground cumin

1 (28-ounce) can crushed tomatoes

1 (12-ounce) package Beyond,
   Impossible, or Sweet Earth brand
   ground "meat"

1 (15.5-ounce) can black beans,
   drained and rinsed

1 (15-ounce) can kidney beans, drained
   and rinsed

½ cup water or vegetable
   broth (optional)

Salt

Freshly ground black pepper

Chopped fresh chives, for garnish

Sliced radishes, for garnish

This chili is packed with plant-based protein from black beans, kidney beans, and ground "meat." It brings the heat thanks to the chili powder and jalapeño pepper. Feel free to swap the jalapeño with a hotter variety, such as serrano or habanero, if you can handle it. Top the chili with shredded cheese or sour cream to offset the heat and add some sliced radishes for crunch. Serve with crusty bread for dipping.

1. In a stockpot over medium heat, combine 1 tablespoon of olive oil, the onion, and garlic. Sauté for 3 to 4 minutes, or until the onion is fragrant. Stir in the jalapeño and carrots. Cook for 2 minutes.

2. Add the tomato paste, chili powder, and cumin. Stir to incorporate. Cook for 1 minute.

3. Stir in the crushed tomatoes. Cover the pot and turn the heat to low.

4. In a skillet over medium heat, heat the remaining ¼ teaspoon of olive oil. Add the "meat." Cook for about 7 minutes, breaking it up with a spoon to brown. Add the cooked "meat" to the stockpot.

5. Stir in the black beans and kidney beans. Increase the heat to medium and simmer the chili for 5 minutes. If the chili seems too thick, stir in the water to loosen it up. Taste and season with salt and pepper. Serve garnished with chives and radish slices.

6. Refrigerate leftovers in an airtight container for up to 3 days.

CONTINUED

SPICY BEAN CHILI
CONTINUED

SUBSTITUTION You can exchange the plant-based ground "meat" for three crumbled veggie burgers (any variety) or for one brick of crumbled tempeh. It can also be left out completely and replaced with another can of beans.

PER SERVING Calories: 279; Total fat: 4g; Carbohydrates: 42g; Fiber: 14g; Protein: 21g; Calcium: 107mg; Vitamin D: 0mcg; Vitamin B12: 0mcg; Iron: 6mg; Zinc: 2mg

Heart-Healthy Results

Following a vegetarian diet has been associated with improved health outcomes that include lower levels of obesity, a reduced risk of heart disease, as well as lowered blood pressure. Vegetarians tend to consume more fiber, potassium, and vitamin C than non-vegetarians, which may contribute to the health benefits associated with a meat-free diet.

Chapter Eight

Anytime Eggs

SPICY PESTO DEVILED EGGS

SERVES 10
PREP TIME: 15 minutes
COOK TIME: 15 minutes

10 large eggs

1 teaspoon salt

1 teaspoon baking soda

2 cups arugula

1 jalapeño pepper, seeded

¼ cup toasted pine nuts

6 tablespoons olive oil, plus more as
   needed, divided

1 avocado, peeled and pitted

½ cup plain Greek yogurt

Juice of ½ lemon

½ teaspoon paprika

It's useful to have a tasty deviled egg recipe on hand. They are great for potlucks, appetizers, or just a high-protein snack. These small bites are flavored with a dollop of jalapeño arugula pesto for rich flavor with a little kick. We highly recommend finishing with smoked paprika. It is a favorite of ours and adds a smoky complexity to the eggs. Pesto provides a flavor dimension not found in regular deviled eggs. By using Greek yogurt and avocado, it also cuts down on the saturated fat that deviled eggs typically have. Chances are, they will disappear quickly!

1. Place the eggs in a large pot. Fill the pot with water to cover the eggs by 1 to 2 inches. Add the salt and baking soda (this helps the peeling process). Place the pot over high heat and bring the water to a rapid boil. Turn off the heat and cover the pot. Let the pot sit for 12 minutes on the warm burner.

2. In a food processor, combine the arugula, jalapeño, pine nuts, and 5 tablespoons of olive oil. Blend until well combined. If the pesto looks dry, add more olive oil, 1 tablespoon at a time, until it reaches a smooth consistency. Set aside.

3. When the eggs are finished, immediately drain them and place the eggs in a large pot of ice water for about 5 minutes. This will stop the cooking process and cool them enough to peel.

4. Once the eggs are cool, peel them under slowly running water, which helps remove the shell.

5. Halve the eggs lengthwise and pop out the yolks into a bowl. Place the egg whites onto a platter.

6. To the yolks, add the avocado, yogurt, and lemon juice. Using a fork, mash the yolks until well combined and transfer to a plastic zip-top bag. Snip a bottom corner off the bag. Gently squeeze the bag, as if using a pastry bag, to pipe the filling into the egg whites

7. Garnish with a dollop of pesto and a sprinkling of paprika.

MAKE IT EASIER If you are bringing these eggs to a gathering to share, we recommend bringing the eggs hollowed out already with separate containers of the filling, pesto, and paprika. They will look more presentable if they are put together at the event rather than transporting them already filled.

PER SERVING Calories: 197; Total fat: 18g; Carbohydrates: 3g; Fiber: 1g; Protein: 8g; Calcium: 50mg; Vitamin D: 18mcg; Vitamin B12: 1mcg; Iron: 1mg; Zinc: 1mg

CACIO E PEPE

SERVES 4
PREP TIME: 10 minutes
COOK TIME: 16 minutes

4 large eggs, cold

Salt

1 pound spaghetti

1 tablespoon butter

1 garlic clove, minced

½ cup grated Parmesan cheese, plus more for garnish (optional)

Freshly ground black pepper

¼ cup fresh parsley, chopped

Cacio e pepe means "cheese and pepper," and that is precisely what this simple Italian pasta recipe delivers. The cracked pepper provides sharp flavor, and the Parmesan delivers rich creaminess. But this version has the added benefit of protein from the soft-boiled egg on top. Initially, it may seem a little strange to put an egg over pasta, but try it and you will see why it works so well. The runny yolk adds richness to the cheese, and the pepper tastes spectacular with everything.

1. Bring a large saucepan of water to a boil over medium heat. Carefully lower the eggs into the boiling water and cook them for 6 minutes. Immediately remove the eggs from the water and transfer to a bowl of ice water to cool.

2. Bring a large pot of water to a boil over high heat. Salt the water and cook the pasta according to the package directions. Drain, reserving 1 cup of pasta water for later use.

3. In a skillet over medium heat, melt the butter. Add the garlic and sauté for 1 minute until fragrant. Set aside.

4. Place the drained pasta back into the pot and stir in the Parmesan cheese, sautéed garlic, and a liberal amount of pepper. If the pasta seems too dry, add a little pasta water.

5. Carefully peel the soft-boiled eggs under warm running water.

CONTINUED

6. Plate the pasta and top each serving with a soft-boiled egg. Garnish with parsley and more Parmesan, if desired.
7. Refrigerate leftovers in an airtight container for 3 to 5 days.

MIX IT UP This basic pasta can be modified for personal tastes. Mushrooms are a flavorful addition, or crushed walnuts will add a little crunch. This dish is deliciously simple but feel free to jazz it up if you get inspired.

PER SERVING Calories: 571; Total fat: 13g; Carbohydrates: 85g; Fiber: 4g; Protein: 26g; Calcium: 190mg; Vitamin D: 20mcg; Vitamin B12: 1mcg; Iron: 5mg; Zinc: 3mg

HUEVOS RANCHEROS STUFFED POBLANOS

SERVES 6
PREP TIME: 10 minutes
COOK TIME: 30 minutes

3 large poblano peppers, halved
    lengthwise and seeded

1 teaspoon olive oil

1 onion, diced

1 jalapeño pepper, diced small

1 (15.5-ounce) can black beans,
    drained and rinsed

6 large eggs

1 cup shredded Cheddar cheese

30 tortilla chips

1 large tomato, diced

1 cup salsa

¼ fresh cilantro leaves, chopped

SUBSTITUTION If you don't have poblano
peppers, bell peppers can be used. It
will take extra time to cook due to the
size difference, but they are also tasty
when stuffed this way. Just cook until
the peppers are soft.

This zesty breakfast is a riff on huevos rancheros, a traditional Mexican breakfast of fried eggs served over a charred tortilla. Here, a poblano pepper is filled with a black bean mixture, and the egg is baked right inside the pepper. Tortilla strips are served alongside or crumbled on top for crunch.

1. Preheat the oven to 350° F. Line a baking sheet with parchment paper.
2. Place the poblano pepper halves cut-side up on the prepared baking sheet.
3. In a skillet over medium heat, heat the olive oil. Add the onion and jalapeño. Sauté for 3 to 4 minutes, stirring frequently, or until the onion is fragrant. Stir in the black beans and sauté for 4 minutes. Transfer the mixture to a bowl and mash with a fork. Evenly fill the poblano boats with the bean mixture.
4. Crack an egg into each boat. Top each with a generous amount of cheese.
5. Bake for 15 to 20 minutes, or until the egg whites have set.
6. Serve on a bed of tortilla chips and garnish with tomato, salsa, and cilantro.
7. Refrigerate leftovers in an airtight container for 1 to 2 days.

PER SERVING Calories: 360; Total fat: 18g; Carbohydrates: 34g; Fiber: 7g; Protein: 18g; Calcium: 218mg; Vitamin D: 20mcg; Vitamin B12: 1mcg; Iron: 3mg; Zinc: 2mg

6. Pour chowder into each bowl, over the egg. Garnish with Parmesan.

7. Refrigerate leftover chowder, cooled, in an airtight container for 3 to 4 days. We recommend poaching the eggs right before you serve the chowder.

MAKE IT EASIER If you find poaching eggs difficult, a soft-boiled egg suits this recipe as well. Just boil an egg for 6 minutes, cool it in an ice bath, and peel. You will still get the runny egg yolk, which is the key to this delicious recipe.

PER SERVING Calories: 300; Total fat: 11g; Carbohydrates: 42g; Fiber: 5g; Protein: 13g; Calcium: 104mg; Vitamin D: 36mcg; Vitamin B12: 1mcg; Iron: 2mg; Zinc: 2mg

BROCCOLI MUSHROOM BREAKFAST PIZZA WITH SALSA VERDE

SERVES 6
PREP TIME: 15 minutes
COOK TIME: 25 minutes

1 tablespoon olive oil

12 tomatillos, husked, washed well, and halved

2 jalapeño peppers

3 garlic cloves, peeled

1 bunch fresh cilantro, plus more for garnish

Prebaked pizza crust of choice

1 cup shredded Cheddar cheese

1 cup diced mushrooms

1 cup diced broccoli

3 large eggs

There is no better time for pizza than breakfast, especially when you add zesty salsa verde, veggies, and eggs. To start your day right, the broccoli provides iron, which aids your body in the transport of oxygen in the red blood cells, as well as being a good source of fiber and vitamins C and K. The mushrooms also contain protein, vitamins, minerals, and antioxidants. But above all, they provide scrumptious flavor, with the green salsa adding a little heat. Enjoy this healthy pizza morning, noon, or night.

1. Preheat the oven to broil.
2. Coat a baking sheet with the olive oil. Place the tomatillos, cut-side down, whole jalapeños, and garlic cloves on the prepared baking sheet. Broil for 10 minutes, or until the tomatillos are dark brown. Remove from the broiler and let cool slightly. Cut the stems off the jalapeños and transfer them to a blender. Add the tomatillos, garlic, and cilantro. Pulse until only small chunks remain to make the salsa verde.
3. Preheat the oven to 400° F.
4. Spoon a thin layer of salsa verde over the pizza crust. Add the cheese, mushrooms, and broccoli, scattering them around the crust.
5. Crack the eggs, one at a time, and place them on the pizza, evenly spaced.

CONTINUED

BROCCOLI MUSHROOM BREAKFAST
PIZZA WITH SALSA VERDE
CONTINUED

6. Place the pizza directly on the oven rack and bake for 10 to 15 minutes, or until the eggs are set and the cheese has slightly browned. Garnish with cilantro and serve immediately.

7. Refrigerate leftovers in an airtight container for 1 day.

MAKE IT EASIER Use a store-bought salsa verde to reduce prep time. If you are unable to track down green salsa, any red salsa will also work. Hot sauce is also a tasty addition to this flavorful breakfast pizza.

PER SERVING Calories: 221; Total fat: 12g; Carbohydrates: 18g; Fiber: 4g; Protein: 12g; Calcium: 167mg; Vitamin D: 13mcg; Vitamin B12: 1mcg; Iron: 2mg; Zinc: 2mg

Strength in Numbers

There are six to eight million adults in the United States who are vegetarian or vegan, according to a 2016 Harris Interactive poll. About two million are vegan, avoiding all animal products, including milk, cheese, and eggs. Additionally, several million others report having eliminated red meat but still consume chicken or fish.

JACKFRUIT PAPRIKASH
WITH BAKED EGGS

SERVES 6
PREP TIME: 15 minutes
COOK TIME: 40 minutes

1 tablespoon olive oil

1 red onion, diced

3 garlic cloves, minced

1 (20-ounce) can young jackfruit, drained and diced

1 bell pepper, any color, sliced

2 cups chopped mushrooms

3 tablespoons paprika

1 teaspoons garlic powder

½ cup dry red wine

2 plum tomatoes, diced

1 tablespoon tomato paste

1½ cups vegetable broth

½ cup sour cream

¼ cup fresh parsley leaves, chopped, plus more for garnish

4 large eggs

The rich and savory Hungarian sauce in this dish highlights the jackfruit and mushrooms splendidly. The baked eggs add an element of delicacy. Paprikash is classically made with chicken. In this vegetarian version, the mushrooms and jackfruit provide great texture to replace the traditional meat. If you cannot find jackfruit, use extra-firm tofu or tempeh. The deep flavors achieved by the red wine and spice blend are what make this dish a winner. Use fresh paprika—sweet or hot Hungarian paprika tastes best for this classic recipe. Serve over rice, egg noodles, or another grain, as desired.

1. Preheat the oven to 400° F.

2. In a deep, heavy-bottomed, oven-safe skillet over medium heat, heat the olive oil. Add the red onion and sauté for 2 minutes. Add the garlic and cook for 2 minutes, stirring to combine.

3. Add the jackfruit to the skillet and cook for 7 to 8 minutes, until lightly browned on all sides. Add the bell pepper and cook for 4 minutes, stirring occasionally.

4. Add the mushrooms to the skillet. Cook, stirring occasionally, for 7 to 8 minutes, until the mushrooms have softened. Stir in the paprika and garlic powder.

5. Stir in the red wine, tomatoes, tomato paste, and vegetable broth. Cook for about 10 minutes, stirring occasionally, until thickened. Stir in the sour cream and parsley.

CONTINUED

6. Using the back of a spoon, make 4 holes in the paprikash. Crack an egg into each hole. Cover the skillet and place it in the oven for 7 to 10 minutes, until the whites are firm, but the yolks are still runny. Garnish with parsley and serve.

7. Refrigerate leftovers in an airtight container for 2 to 3 days.

ANIMAL STYLE Baked or roast chicken can be added to this recipe. Simply cook it separately and add the chicken when serving for anyone who prefers to have meat.

PER SERVING Calories: 202; Total fat: 10g; Carbohydrates: 25g; Fiber: 3g; Protein: 7g; Calcium: 77mg; Vitamin D: 16mcg; Vitamin B12: 1mcg; Iron: 2mg; Zinc: 1mg

Chapter Nine

Hearty Mains

BARBECUE CHICKPEA AND CARAMELIZED ONION PITA PIZZAS

SERVES 4
PREP TIME: 10 minutes
COOK TIME: 35 minutes

2 tablespoons olive oil

3 large onions, very thinly sliced

1 (15.5-ounce) can chickpeas, drained and rinsed

1½ cups barbecue sauce, divided

4 pita breads

1½ cups shredded Gouda cheese

¼ cup chopped fresh cilantro leaves

Pita pizza is an easy alternative to the calorie-dense classic. It's easier and faster to prepare and it is personal size, which allows everyone in the house to create their own special pizza. For this recipe, the chickpeas are coated in a sweet and spicy barbecue sauce and placed over a bed of caramelized onions, creating a savory combination. Topped with Gouda and fresh cilantro, it's a flavorful meal everyone is sure to enjoy.

1. Preheat the oven to 375° F.
2. In a large skillet over medium-low heat, combine the olive oil and the onion. Sauté for 15 minutes, stirring frequently, or until the onions are fully browned but not burned. Remove from the skillet and set aside.
3. Place the skillet over medium heat, add the chickpeas, and cook for 3 to 4 minutes, stirring constantly. The chickpeas should brown slightly.
4. Stir in ¾ cup of barbecue sauce. Simmer for about 5 minutes, stirring frequently, until the sauce becomes very thick. Set aside.
5. Place the pitas on a baking sheet. Add a thin layer of barbecue sauce to each, followed by equal amounts of the Gouda, caramelized onions, and chickpeas.
6. Bake for 7 to 10 minutes, or until the cheese has melted and pitas are golden brown. Top with cilantro and serve.

7. Refrigerate any leftover chickpeas and caramelized onions separately in airtight containers for 3 to 4 days. Use in salads or for sandwiches.

ANIMAL STYLE This meal is perfect for pleasing everyone in the family. Chicken or pork can easily replace the chickpeas for those who prefer meat and, because they are individualized, everyone can have exactly what they like.

PER SERVING Calories: 668; Total fat: 22g; Carbohydrates: 98g; Fiber: 12g; Protein: 24g; Calcium: 375mg; Vitamin D: 0mcg; Vitamin B12: 2mcg; Iron: 4mg; Zinc: 3mg

COCONUT-CRUSTED TOFU

SERVES 4
PREP TIME: 15 minutes
COOK TIME: 20 minutes

1 (14-ounce) package extra-firm
   tofu, drained and cut into
   ½-inch rectangles
½ cup panko bread crumbs
½ cup shredded coconut
¼ teaspoon garlic powder
¼ teaspoon salt
¼ teaspoon freshly ground
   black pepper
2 large eggs

SUBSTITUTION If you are unable to find panko, regular bread crumbs can be used instead or even a gluten-free variety. Also, the egg can be replaced with a flax meal egg to make this meal completely plant-based.

Tofu, also known as bean curd, is made from soy milk that has been pressed into a solid form. It comes in varying levels of softness, from silken to extra firm. For this recipe, extra-firm tofu is best because it gives a sturdy surface for the coconut-panko mixture to adhere to and it produces a dense plant-based cutlet perfect for baking. This coconut-crusted tofu is easy, delicious, and healthy. Serve it with a mustard sauce for dipping or a fresh salad for a light meal.

1. Preheat the oven to 400° F. Line a baking sheet with parchment paper.
2. Place the tofu on paper towels to absorb some of the excess water.
3. In a shallow bowl, stir together the bread crumbs, coconut, garlic powder, salt, and pepper. In another shallow bowl, whisk the eggs.
4. One at a time, dip each piece of tofu first into the egg and next into the coconut mixture, coating each piece well. Place the coated tofu on the prepared baking sheet as each is finished.
5. Bake the tofu for 15 to 20 minutes, or until golden brown, flipping once about halfway through the baking time.
6. Refrigerate leftovers in an airtight container for 3 to 4 days.

PER SERVING Calories: 216; Total fat: 12g; Carbohydrates: 14g; Fiber: 2g; Protein: 15 g; Calcium: 213mg; Vitamin D: 9mcg; Vitamin B12: 2mcg; Iron: 4mg; Zinc: 2mg

LEMON TOFU OVER SAUTÉED KALE

SERVES 4
PREP TIME: 10 minutes
COOK TIME: 15 minutes

1 (14-ounce) package extra-firm tofu

2 teaspoons olive oil, divided

4 cups stemmed and chopped kale

3 garlic cloves, minced

1 cup vegetable broth, divided

1 tablespoon cornstarch

¼ cup honey

2 tablespoons soy sauce

Juice of 1 lemon

Zest of 1 lemon

Salt

Freshly ground black pepper

Lemon is an underrated fruit that doesn't always get the credit it deserves. It's zippy and bright and goes great with just about everything. It's also packed with vitamin C and supports overall good health. The tofu in this recipe is pan-fried, then coated with a sweet lemony glaze. Finally, the tofu is placed on a bed of vitamin-rich kale. Raw kale tends to be tough to eat, but, when sautéed, it goes down easily. Serve alone or with a side of rice and garnish with extra lemon zest and fresh basil, if desired.

1. Press the excess water out of the tofu using paper towels, then cube the tofu into bite-size pieces.

2. In a large skillet over high heat, combine 1 teaspoon of olive oil and the tofu. Cook, stirring frequently, for 7 to 8 minutes, until all sides are golden brown. Remove from the skillet and set aside.

3. Return the skillet to medium heat and add the remaining 1 teaspoon of olive oil. Add the kale and garlic. Sauté for 2 to 3 minutes, stirring frequently, until the kale has wilted. Remove from the skillet and set aside.

4. In a small bowl, whisk ¼ cup vegetable broth and the cornstarch until the cornstarch dissolves. Set aside.

5. Place the skillet over medium heat and add the remaining ¾ cup of vegetable broth, the honey, soy sauce, and lemon juice. Bring the mixture to a simmer, stirring occasionally. Reduce the heat to low and stir in the lemon zest and cornstarch mixture. Cook, stirring constantly, until the sauce begins to thicken.

6. Add the tofu and cook, stirring constantly, for 2 to 3 minutes until the tofu is warm and well coated. Plate the sautéed kale and top with the lemon tofu. Season with salt and pepper, as desired.

7. Refrigerate leftovers in an airtight container for 3 to 4 days.

MIX IT UP This pan-fried tofu can also be adapted for other sauces and seasonings. It can be coated in a spicy chili garlic sauce, or seasonings can simply be added to the cooked tofu for a dry-rub version.

PER SERVING Calories: 233; Total fat: 9g; Carbohydrates: 30g; Fiber: 2g; Protein: 14g; Calcium: 273mg; Vitamin D: 0mcg; Vitamin B12: 2mcg; Iron: 3mg; Zinc: 2mg

6. Remove the potatoes and the barbecue sauce mixture from the oven. Stir the black beans into the barbecue sauce mixture and slice open the potatoes. Fill the potatoes with the barbecue sauce and bean mixture. Garnish with fresh cilantro.

7. Refrigerate any leftover filling in an airtight container for 4 to 5 days. Use for other meals, such as sandwiches or wraps.

MAKE IT EASIER A great way to cut down on the potato baking time is to start it in the microwave for 5 to 10 minutes, then move it to the oven so the skin gets nice and crispy. If you have an Instant Pot or other electric pressure cooker, you can cook potatoes using the pressure cook setting for 12 minutes. But don't forget to poke holes in the potatoes with a fork before cooking them.

PER SERVING Calories: 551; Total fat: 5g; Carbohydrates: 121g; Fiber: 14g; Protein: 11g; Calcium: 134mg; Vitamin D: 0mcg; Vitamin B12: 1mcg; Iron: 4mg; Zinc: 2mg

Creamy, dreamy mac and
cheese waiting to be baked to
golden-brown perfection.

BAKED MAC AND CHEESE

SERVES 8
PREP TIME: 10 minutes
COOK TIME: 1 hour, 10 minutes

1 pound dried elbow macaroni
½ cup (1 stick) butter, plus more for the baking dish
3 tablespoons all-purpose flour
2 quarts milk
4 cups shredded extra-sharp Cheddar cheese

MAKE IT EASIER This mac and cheese can be prepared in advance, refrigerated, and baked later, or it can be baked and frozen to be reheated and eaten later. Your taste buds will be none the wiser, and it tastes just as good on a later day as it did on the first.

Macaroni and cheese is classic American comfort food. This traditional recipe is made with extra-sharp cheese for even more flavor. This recipe serves a crowd, which is great if you have young or finicky eaters. It can also be modified to include sautéed greens or veggies for a healthy twist, or bread crumbs can be sprinkled on top for a bit of texture. This classic will not disappoint and will have you coming back for more.

1. Bring a large pot of salted water to a boil over high heat. Add the macaroni and cook according to the package directions.
2. Preheat the oven to 350° F. Coat an extra-large oven-safe casserole dish with butter. Set aside.
3. While the macaroni cooks, in a large saucepan over medium-low heat, melt the butter. Add the flour, whisking constantly to prevent burning and to form a roux. Cook for about 2 minutes.
4. Add the milk and cook for 3 to 4 minutes, stirring constantly, until the mixture becomes thick and bubbly. Add the cheese and stir until melted.
5. Drain the pasta and transfer to the prepared dish. Add the cheese mixture and stir until well combined.
6. Bake for 50 to 60 minutes, or until heated through and nicely browned.
7. Serve warm.
8. Refrigerate leftovers, covered, for 4 to 5 days.

PER SERVING Calories: 673; Total fat: 36g; Carbohydrates: 58g; Fiber: 2g; Protein: 30g; Calcium: 709mg; Vitamin D: 120mcg; Vitamin B12: 2mcg; Iron: 1mg; Zinc: 4mg

EGGPLANT AND BUTTERNUT MARSALA

SERVES 6
PREP TIME: 15 minutes
COOK TIME: 30 minutes

2 tablespoons olive oil, divided

1 eggplant, sliced crosswise into
   1-inch-thick pieces

1 butternut squash, peeled,
   seeded, and sliced crosswise into
   ½-inch-thick pieces

2 garlic cloves, minced

1 small onion diced

2 pints baby bella mushrooms, sliced

2 tablespoons fresh thyme leaves, plus
   more for garnish (optional)

2 tablespoons flour of choice

1 tablespoon dried parsley

½ teaspoon garlic powder

¼ teaspoon salt

¼ teaspoon freshly ground
   black pepper

1 cup vegetable broth

1 cup Marsala wine

2½ tablespoons butter

This dish simply brims with flavor. For this vegetarian adaptation of the traditional Marsala, the meat, typically chicken or steak, has been replaced with butternut squash and eggplant, which produce a substantial meal minus the meat. The flavorful mushroom sauce is made with Marsala wine, which is a fortified wine produced in the Marsala region of Sicily. It can be found at most grocery stores near the olive oil. Serve with rice, pasta, or polenta, as desired.

1. Preheat the oven to 400° F. Coat two baking sheets with 1 teaspoon olive oil each.

2. Place the eggplant and squash slices in a single layer on the prepared baking sheets. Brush the tops of the vegetables with 1 teaspoon olive oil. Bake for 15 to 20 minutes, flipping the vegetables halfway through the baking time, until golden brown on both sides.

3. In a deep skillet over medium heat, heat the remaining 1 tablespoon of olive oil. Add the garlic and onion and sauté for about 2 minutes, or until fragrant. Add the mushrooms and thyme. Cook, stirring frequently, for 5 to 7 minutes, until the mushrooms start to brown.

4. Stir in the flour, parsley, garlic powder, salt, and pepper to coat the mushrooms lightly and as evenly as possible. Add the vegetable broth and wine to the skillet. Cook for about 3 minutes, stirring occasionally, until the liquid begins to thicken. Add the butter, stirring to incorporate, until the butter melts.

5. Serve the eggplant and squash topped with the mushroom sauce. Garnish with more fresh thyme, if desired.
6. Refrigerate leftovers in an airtight container for up to 5 days.

ANIMAL STYLE   The mushroom sauce can easily be drizzled over cooked chicken or steak. Prepare the meat separately and spoon some of the sauce over the protein instead of the roasted squash and eggplant.

PER SERVING Calories: 234; Total fat: 10g; Carbohydrates: 28g; Fiber: 7g; Protein: 5 g; Calcium: 83mg; Vitamin D: 3mcg; Vitamin B12: 0mcg; Iron: 2mg; Zinc: 1mg

Freshly cooked pumpkin gnocchi is beautiful on its own, but delicious when topped with decadent cashew cream sauce.

	Raw / Cooked	Cooking Methods	Serving Ideas
	Raw / cooked	Braise; grill; sauté; simmer; roast; stir-fry; steam	Warm or raw salad; raw slaws; soup; ramen; add to grain, vegetable, and legume dishes; raw with a dip for an appetizer; pickled; add to a green smoothie
	Raw / cooked	Bake; blanch; braise; fry; grill; roast; sauté; simmer; steam; stir-fry; slow cooker; pressure cooker	Add to egg dishes, such as casseroles and quiche; roast with olive oil, smoked paprika, salt, and pepper, and finish with lemon juice; stir-fry with other vegetables in sesame oil, and finish with soy sauce; add to raw salads, Buddha bowls, grains, legumes, and vegetable casseroles; roast and toss with pasta, capers, preserved lemon, grated Parmesan cheese, and toasted breadcrumbs; soup; add roasted broccoli to pizza toppings
	Raw / cooked	Roast; bake; steam; braise; fry; sauté; grill; pressure cooker; slow cooker	Slice thinly for a raw salad with green onions and dried cranberries; roast with apples; make a hash with potatoes, onion, and apple cider vinegar; toss with garlic, spices, and olive oil and throw on the grill; bake into a cheesy gratin
	Cooked	Roast; sauté; steam; simmer; slow cooker; pressure cooker	Stuff with grains and/or vegetables; spiralize into pasta; add to salads, grains, legumes, and vegetables; soup; risotto
	Raw / cooked	Roast; braise; sauté; steam; grill; bake; stir-fry; slow cooker	Roast wedges rubbed with olive oil, garlic paste, salt, and pepper; braise red cabbage with olive oil, cider vinegar, brown sugar, and apple chunks; slaw; cabbage rolls stuffed with rice and vegetables; pickle for kimchi; topping for tacos
	Raw / cooked	Roast; braise; sauté; steam; grill; bake; stir-fry; slow cooker; pressure cooker; simmer; steam	Raw in a salad; soup; slaw; soufflé; bread; cake; add to vegetable, grain, and legume dishes; simmer in a pan with butter, honey, and orange juice until all the liquid is gone except a glaze
	Raw / cooked	Bake; blanch; braise; fry; grill; roast; sauté; simmer; steam; stir-fry; pressure cooker; slow cooker	Purée into a sauce; grate into rice for tabbouleh or risotto; roast whole, smothered with a spicy sauce; substitute it for chicken in many dishes; soup; pickle for kimchi; swap out potatoes in mashed potatoes; use in a gratin; toss with pasta, lemon, capers, and breadcrumbs

	Prepping Options	Tools	
Celery	Trim bottoms; cut into long strips or dice	Chef's knife	
Corn	Remove kernels by standing a cob up in a bowl lined with a towel; anchor it with one hand, and slide a knife down the cob to slice off the kernels	Chef's knife	
Cucumber	Peel, halve, and scrape out juicy seeds; cut into thin or thick slices, peel into long ribbons, dice, grate, or pickle	Vegetable peeler; chef's knife; paring knife; spoon; box grater	
Delicata squash	Slice off the ends, halve, and scrape out the seeds; cut into half-moons or purée	Chef's knife; spoon; food processor or blender	
Eggplant	Slice off the ends, cut into ¾-inch slices, sprinkle evenly with salt, lay in a colander to drain for 30 minutes, then rinse to remove the salt and pat dry; slice, chop, dice, mash, or purée	Chef's knife; colander	
Garlic	Peel, chop the bulbs, and thinly slice, mince, or smash and lightly salt to form a paste	Chef's knife	
Ginger	Peel with a spoon and trim; slice, mince, or grate	Spoon; paring knife; fine grater or zester	
Green beans	Trim; slice lengthwise or crosswise on the diagonal	Paring knife; chef's knife	

	Raw / Cooked	Cooking Methods	Serving Ideas
	Raw / cooked	Roast; braise; sauté; bake; stir-fry; simmer	Use for making stock; soffritto; make a celery gratin; braise in broth with tomatoes and onions and top with shavings of Parmesan; add to salads for crunch
	Raw / cooked	Sauté; roast; simmer; steam; grill	Chowder; stew; add to tacos with black beans, tomatoes, and avocado with a squeeze of lime; sauté with pickled onion, basil, and tomatoes and stuff into peppers with a little cheese; risotto; toss with zoodles, mint, and tomatoes; make Mexican corn
	Raw / cooked	Sauté; bake; stir-fry	Use in salads, especially Greek and Middle Eastern salads; make tzatziki; swap out bread for cucumber disks; pickled; chilled soup; make a sandwich with cream cheese and dill; add slices to jugs of water; sauté with a little butter, salt, pepper, scallions, and mint
	Cooked	Roast; bake; sauté; simmer; grill; braise; steam; slow cooker; pressure cooker; stir-fry	Soup; stuff scooped-out half with grains, dried fruits, and other vegetables; drizzle with oil and garlic, sprinkle with salt, pepper, and cayenne, and roast; add to warm salads or Buddha bowls; use as a pizza topping; toss with pasta; add to tacos; purée to add to chilis and stews; bake into a gratin
	Cooked	Bake; roast; sauté; simmer; grill; stir-fry; braise; slow cooker; pressure cooker	Mash into a dip such as baba ghanoush; marinate and grill for a sandwich with tomatoes and smoked mozzarella; lightly bread and bake in a tomato sauce topped with Parmesan; roast and stuff with a grains and pomegranate seed salad; simmer with tomatoes, onion, garlic, and balsamic vinegar and puree for a soup
	Raw / cooked	Roast; sauté; blanch; bake; stir-fry	Drizzle a garlic head with olive oil and wrap in foil with a rosemary sprig and roast; sauté or roast chopped or thinly sliced garlic with vegetables, legumes, or grains; add to a soup with onions and thyme
	Raw / cooked	Simmer; sauté; stir-fry	Tea; add to broths and soups; grate finely to add to fruit with a squeeze of fresh lime; add to miso and garlic paste to rub on vegetables; gingerbread; add to sauces or jams
	Cooked	Blanch; sauté; simmer; bake; roast; stir-fry	Add to salads, soups, and grains; roast with olive oil, thyme, salt, pepper, and a squeeze of lemon

	Prepping Options	Tools	
Jalapeño peppers, serrano chiles	Trim off the stem, halve, and remove the seeds and pith; slice, dice, or mince	Paring knife	
Kale	Fold leaves over the central tough rib, and remove the rib with a knife (not necessary for baby kale); coarsely chop	Chef's knife	
Leeks	Cut and discard the top part of the leek with tough, dark green leaves, halve lengthwise, and feather under cold running water to remove dirt; cut into thin half-moons	Chef's knife	
Mango	Slice "cheeks" of mango off from stem to end, parallel and as close as possible to the long, flat pit; score the cheeks down to, but not through, the skin using the tip of a sharp knife; turn the cheek 90 degrees and score again; scoop out the mango chunks using a spoon; purée	Paring knife; food processor or blender	
Mushrooms, small	Wipe clean with a paper towel and slice, quarter, or mince	Chef's knife	
Olives (green, Niçoise, Kalamata)	Slice, smash using the flat side of a chef's knife, coarsely chop, or leave whole	Chef's knife	
Onion, shallot	Chop, dice, grate, or slice	Chef's knife	
Parsley and cilantro	Position a sharp knife at a 45-degree angle to the herbs and slice across the leaves to coarsely chop, including stems; gather the leaves and stems together and chop into smaller pieces or continue chopping to mince	Chef's knife	

Index

About
the Authors

Alissa Bilden Warham and **Steve Warham** are the founders of the plant-based food and drink blog Meatless Makeovers, which specializes in recreating traditional recipes they grew up with for a meat-free diet. They develop, cook, and photograph every recipe on the site. Alissa is a teacher who finds joy in helping others achieve their goals, and Steve is a professional photographer. Alissa grew up in Montana and Steve was raised in upstate New York, where meat was a staple in both their diets. Now they live in Brooklyn with their cat, Gertrude, and find recipe inspiration from the diverse cultures and cuisines of New York City. To find more creative and satisfying meatless recipes, visit their blog: meatlessmakeovers.com.